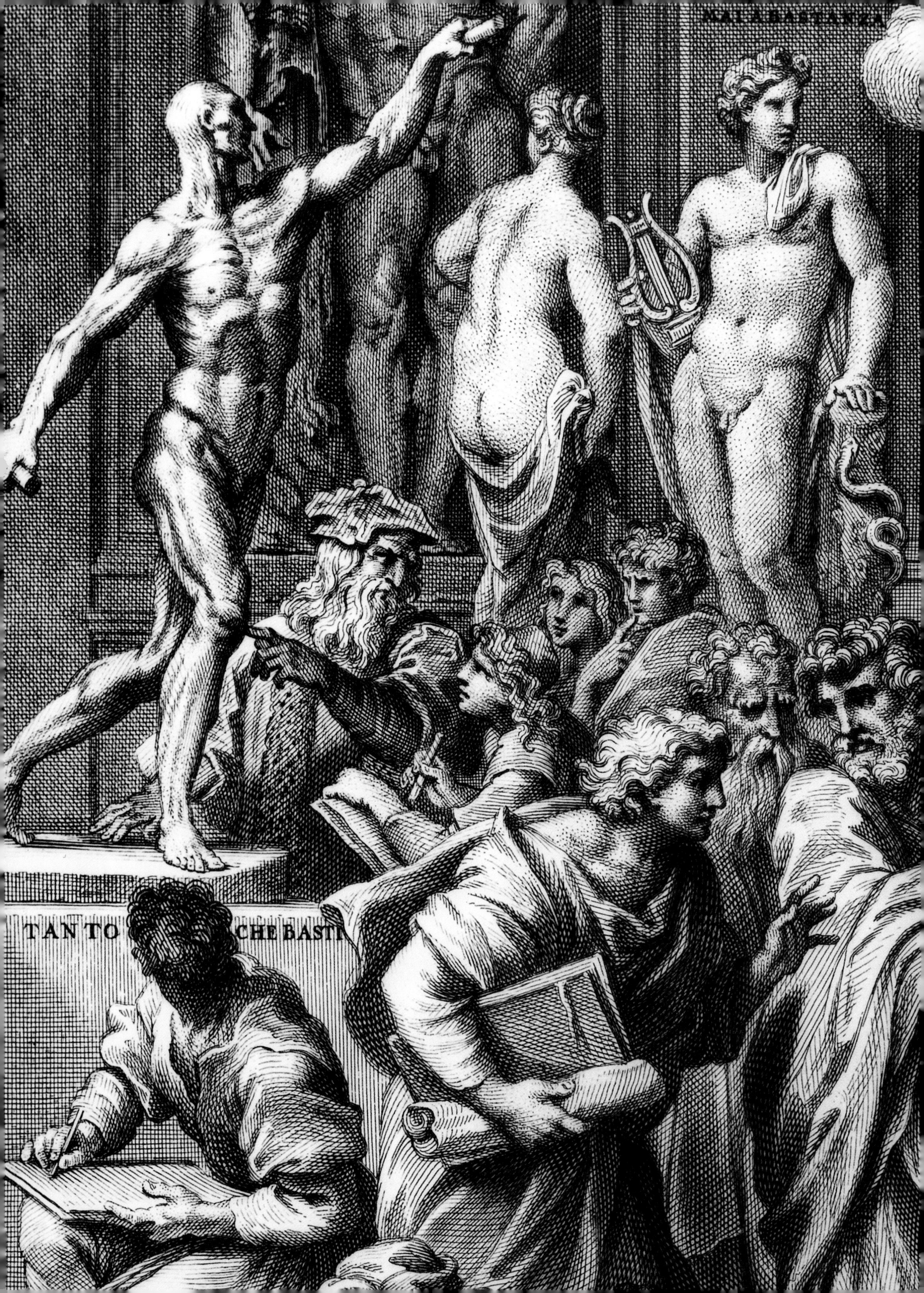
MALA BASTANZA
TANTO CHE BASTI

Antiquity in Rome

from the Renaissance to the Age of Enlightenment

Selections from Dartmouth's Collections

T. Barton Thurber
Adrian W. B. Randolph

Hood Museum of Art, Dartmouth College

Hood Museum of Art, Dartmouth College
Hanover, New Hampshire 03755

Antiquity in Rome from the Renaissance to the Age of Enlightenment: Selections from Dartmouth's Collections
Hood Museum of Art, Dartmouth College
Hanover, New Hampshire
July 7 to September 9, 2001

This exhibition was organized by the Hood Museum of Art, Dartmouth College. The exhibition and catalogue have been generously funded by the Marie-Louise and Samuel R. Rosenthal Fund and the William Chase Grant 1919 Memorial Fund.

Library of Congress
Cataloging-in-Publication Data

Thurber, T. Barton.
Antiquity in Rome from the Renaissance to the age of enlightenment : selections from Dartmouth's collections / T. Barton Thurber ; Adrian W. B. Randolph.
p. cm.
Exhibition catalog.
Includes bibliographical references.
ISBN 0-944722-23-7 (pbk.)
1. Art, Renaissance—Italy—Rome—Themes, motives—Exhibitions. 2. Art, Baroque—Italy—Rome—Themes, motives—Exhibitions. 3. Classical antiquities in art—Exhibitions. 4. Art—Private collections—New Hampshire—Hanover—Exhibitions. 5. Art—New Hampshire—Hanover—Exhibitions. 6. Dartmouth College—Art collections—Exhibitions. I. Randolph, Adrian W. B., 1965- II. Hood Museum of Art. III. Title.
N6920 .T495 2001
704.9'49937'09450747423—DC21
2001001748

All drawings, prints, paintings, and sculptures owned by the Hood Museum of Art and Dartmouth College were photographed by Jeffrey Nintzel. Other photographs: figure 3, Alinari/Art Resource, N.Y.; figure 5, Giraudon/Art Resource, N.Y.; figure 14, Ali Elai; figure 26, Ed Quinn.

Cover, inside cover, and back inside cover: Giovanni Battista Piranesi, 1720–1778, *View of the Principal Elevation of the Antonine Column* (detail), about 1776, etching, Hood Museum of Art, Dartmouth College; PR.967.130.28

Frontispiece: Nicolas Dorigny, 1652/58–1746, after Carlo Maratta, 1625–1713, *The Academy of Painting* (detail), 1728, engraving, collection of Robert Dance, Class of 1977

Printed by Mercantile/Image Press

Designed by Glenn Suokko

Contents

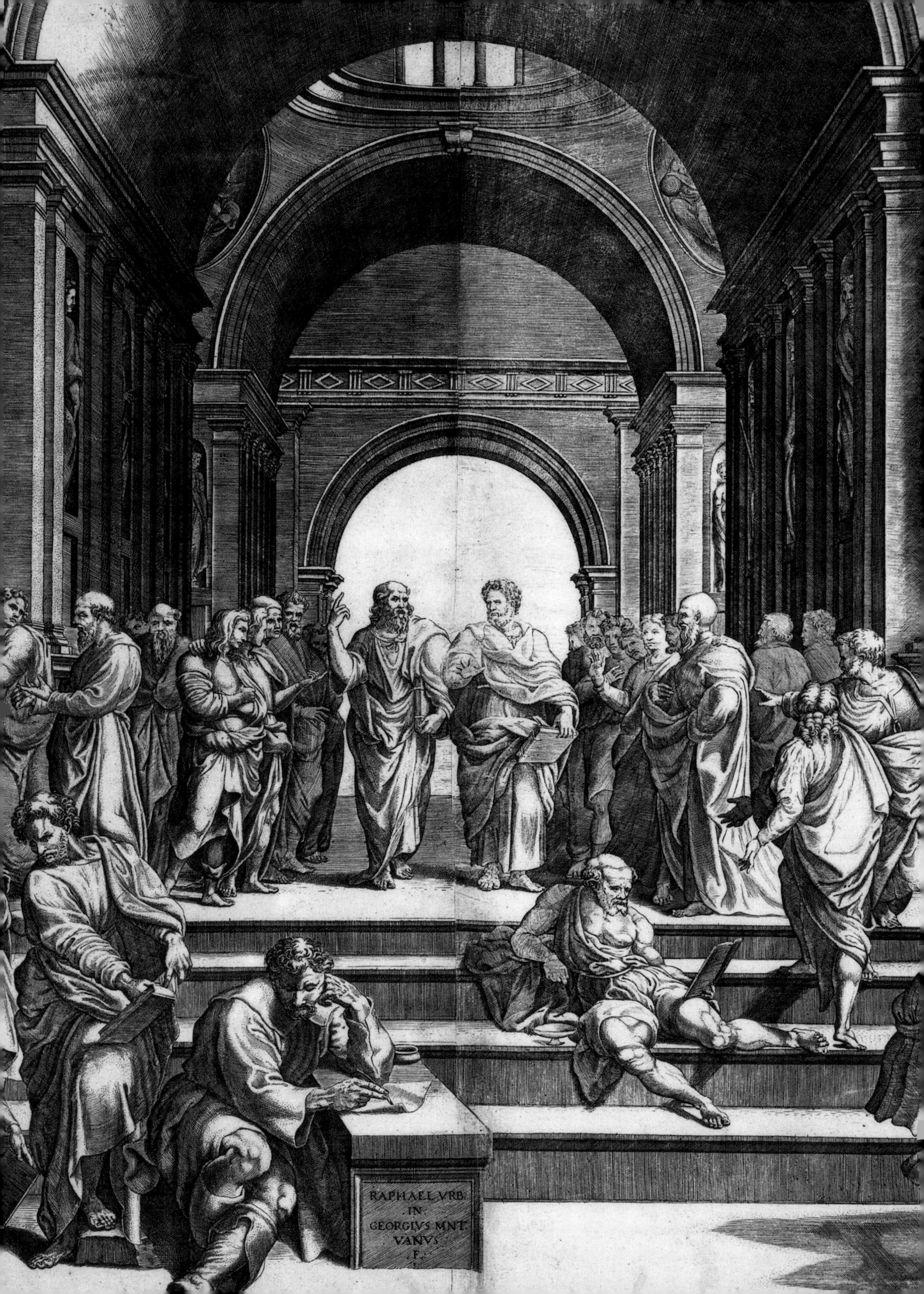
RAPHAEL VRB.
.IN.
GEORGIVS MNT
VANVS
.F.

Introduction

> Can you believe of me that I am wandering about this city of Rome, swivelling my eyes this way and that like some boorish gallant, clambering up palace walls, even up to their windows, on the chance of seeing something of the beauties inside? . . . I am doing all this in the hope of finding in these places beauty not in living bodies but in stones, marbles, and images. (Manuel Chrysoloras, political emissary to the pope, about 1411–12)[1]

THESE COMMENTS STILL convey a vivid sense of the sensory spectacle that Rome promised its visitors near the beginning of the Renaissance. From about this time, and continuing to at least the late eighteenth century, countless travelers ambled along Roman streets, marveling at the architecture, sculptures, and paintings, all reflections of a glorious and worthy past. Manuel Chrysoloras makes it clear that his voyeuristic pursuit of such sights was not driven by base, contemporary concerns—that is, by "living bodies"—but rather by his ardent interest in the ancient marvels around him. Looking for this barely concealed beauty in Rome implied a physical commitment to discovery, an active search that could be undertaken only by someone curious enough to wander into the city's ruined districts, scramble over its crumbling walls, or peer surreptitiously through its uncovered windows. Dignified scholars might eventually be granted limited access to artifacts, but to discover the beautiful immediately and independently was to risk one's reputation. Over the next several centuries, firsthand investigation of these treasures was commonplace on the European Grand Tour, and subsequent visitors were led across a Rome made all too familiar by guidebooks. Serious study of antiquity nevertheless provided the educated elite with an obligatory, if not altogether fresh, set of visual references for historical reflection and self-definition. Thus conceived, Rome's artistic heritage came to be understood as both a lasting measure of high aesthetic standards and an authoritative index of creative accomplishments.

The Hood Museum of Art's exhibition *Antiquity in Rome from the Renaissance to the Age of Enlightenment: Selections from Dartmouth's Collections* reviews this historical trajectory and considers the ways that this widely shared yet topographically specific repertoire of "stones, marbles, and images" was reused and reinterpreted over time. In so doing, the exhibition celebrates a large group of

OPPOSITE:
Giorgio Ghisi, 1520–1582, after Raphael, 1483–1520, *The School of Athens* (detail), 1550, engraving, gift of Jane and W. David Dance, Class of 1940; PR.991.58.1

important works from the museum's permanent collection. The oldest work in the exhibition, a fragment of a Roman sarcophagus, comes down to us from the second century CE, while the most modern image, a fine printed glimpse of sublime ruins, dates to the late eighteenth century. Some key works displayed here first entered Dartmouth's collections early in the twentieth century—for example, Giovanni Battista Piranesi's engraving of the Campo Vaccino—while others have only been acquired in the last twenty years—notably an early seventeenth-century oil painting by Claude Lorrain and, still more recently, Andrea Mantegna's late-fifteenth-century tour de force, *Battle of the Sea Gods*. The exhibition thus provides visitors to the museum with an opportunity to scrutinize the depth and nature of its still evolving European collections. Furthermore, several illustrated texts have been integrated into the exhibition—all from the Special Collections at Dartmouth's Rauner and Sherman libraries—and their presence helps to demonstrate the spread of humanist and popular knowledge through the printed media. Finally, a few objects from selected private collections with close links to the Dartmouth community have also been lent to the exhibition; these works enhance the quality and breadth of the exhibition as a whole, particularly in the case of the sculptural artifacts.

Just as the exposure to Roman monuments in the Renaissance and Baroque periods left lasting impressions on visiting artists such as Hendrik Goltzius and Nicolas Poussin, so do they impress us today—reason enough, we feel, for a project like this one to be undertaken at the beginning of the twenty-first century. Looking "this way and that" at these objects—some decidedly strange, some touchingly familiar—introduces a wider set of issues surrounding these retrospective images. Works of art demand to be understood in relation to certain historical contexts and in response to unique social pressures. Indeed, the sculptures, medals, prints, paintings, books, and drawings presented here were avidly collected, studied, and exchanged by residents and travelers to Rome. In turn, these individuals were themselves deeply implicated in the proliferation of images of the city throughout the Renaissance and Baroque periods. The two essays that follow this introduction provide general overviews of the circumstances that surrounded such representations from the fifteenth through the eighteenth centuries. Pointing at the self-conscious ways in which these images were imaginatively conceived and interpreted as meaningful, the checklist to the exhibition further divides its subject into separate sections. These thematic groupings emphasize the variety of connections people made over time between the images and associated concepts of ancient Rome. Such a division of works suggests a highly nuanced approach to issues of place, memory, status, iconography, aesthetics, and historical imagination. The Hood Museum of Art possesses a strong tradition of such sophisticated curatorial thinking, and *Antiquity in Rome from the Renaissance to the Age of Enlightenment* continues to build upon that solid foundation.

I would like to take this opportunity to express deep appreciation to a number of individuals who have helped to insure the success of this project. In particular, *Antiquity in Rome from the Renaissance to the Age of Enlightenment* provides me with a welcome chance to thank Jean K. Weil, Jane and W. David Dance (Class of '40), and the Hood family once more for recent gifts of art that appear in the checklist to the exhibition. Additionally, I wish to express gratitude to Roger A. Anderson (Class of '68), Robert Dance (Class of '77), and David P. and Barbara

Dau Southwell (Tu '88 and Class of '78), who lent objects from their personal collections to this project; without their generosity and support, the exhibition could not have taken its final form. Additional support for the acquisition of specific works of art appearing in this exhibition has been provided by Peter and Kirsten Bedford, Julia and Richard H. Rush (Class of '37), and William B. Jaffe and Evelyn A. Jaffe Hall. Among our colleagues at Dartmouth College itself, Adrian Randolph, Associate Professor of Art History, deserves thanks for the engaging discussion of Renaissance Rome that he wrote for this catalogue. Philip N. Cronenwett, Special Collections Librarian, shared his expertise, and Stanley W. Brown, Curator of Rare Books, and Barbara E. Reed, Librarian at the Sherman Fine Arts Library, made important texts available for display. At the Hood Museum of Art, I take pride in crediting Juliette Bianco for her administrative skills throughout the planning stages of this project and Nils Nadeau for his admirable attention to the details of this catalogue. Lauren B. Fog (Class of '01), Curatorial Assistant, helped with many administrative details and numerous research problems. Margaret Dyer Chamberlain, the Associate Provost at Dartmouth College, served as Acting Director of the Hood Museum of Art during the early phase of the exhibition's development. As always, I am full of admiration for her thoughtful contributions to this museum before my arrival in Hanover and for her careful stewardship of the institution as a whole. T. Barton Thurber, Curator of European Art, conceived, organized, and executed this project. His scholarly expertise in Italian Baroque art and architecture is evident both in the text he has written and in the works he selected. Most of all, I thank him for his efforts in revealing the ways that the complex allure of Rome—the "eye-swivelling" beauty of its stones, marbles, and images—returns to us through works of art.

Derrick R. Cartwright
Director

Note

1. Manuel Chrysoloras to Demetrius Chrysoloras, quoted in M. Baxandall, *Giotto and the Orators: Humanist Observers of Painting in Italy and the Discovery of Pictorial Composition, 1350–1450* (Oxford: Oxford University Press, 1971), 81.

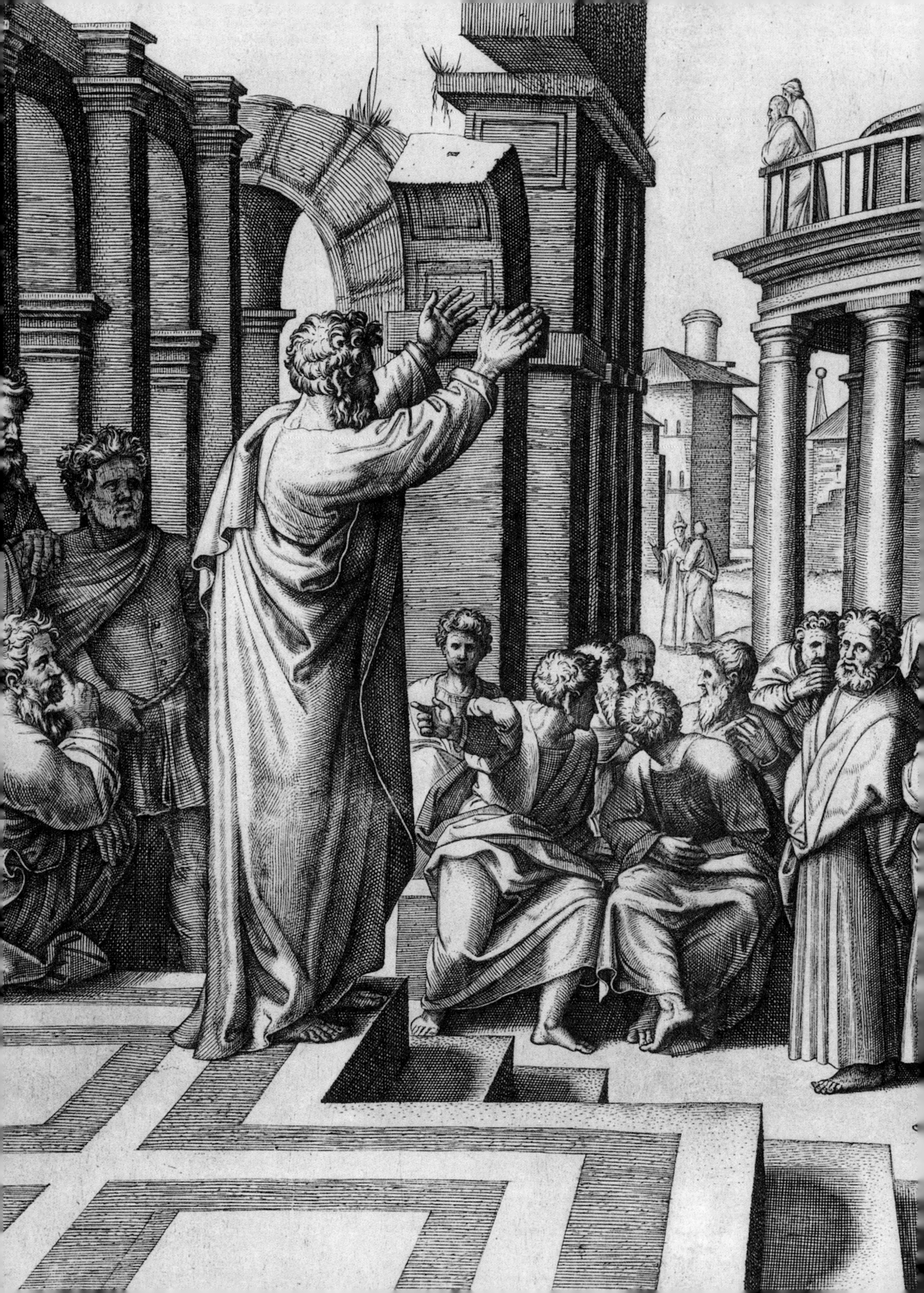

"How Great Rome Was the Ruins Teach": Antiquity in Renaissance Rome

Adrian W. B. Randolph

> When the actual relics of the antique were restored to the world, in the view of the Christian ascetic it was as if an ancient plague-pit had been opened. All the world took the contagion of the life of nature and of the senses. And now it is seen that the medieval spirit too had done something for the new fortunes of the antique. By hastening the decline of art, by withdrawing interest from it and yet keeping unbroken the thread of its traditions, it has suffered the human mind to repose itself, that when day came it might awake, with eyes refreshed, to those ancient, ideal forms.[1]

The nineteenth-century essayist Walter Pater (1839–1894) imagines the horror Christian viewers experienced when confronted with the exhumed relics of pagan culture as that of staring into a charnel pit filled with infectious corporeal remains. The fragmentary bodies of ancient sculpture, Pater fantasizes, could only have appeared horrific to the eyes of the "Christian ascetic." Nonetheless, characterizing the Renaissance viewer, Pater recognizes the profound shift that replaced a medieval unease with the antique and pagan past with "refreshed" eyes, sensible to "those ancient, ideal forms."

Although some scholars have doubted the radical difference between medieval and Renaissance attitudes to which Pater alludes, most agree that fourteenth- and fifteenth-century Europe did witness a transformation of attitude toward pagan antiquity; this transformation was most visible and profound on the Italian peninsula. Here, one could not help confronting remnants of Roman culture—triumphal arches stranded in Italy's cities, ancient tombs dotting the countryside, and rectilinear urban plans reminding medieval inhabitants of their long-dead predecessors. Nowhere, however, was the antique past more legible than in Rome itself. Monuments like the Colosseum, the Pantheon, the Arch of Constantine, the Baths of Diocletian, and Rome's imported Egyptian obelisks stood as mighty and magnificent reminders of past greatness. The known remnants of Roman statuary—the Quirinal *Dioscuri*, the equestrian *Marcus Aurelius*, the *Spinario*, the

OPPOSITE:
Marcantonio Raimondi, about 1470–about 1527, after Raphael, 1483–1520, *Saint Paul Preaching in Athens* (detail), about 1517–20, engraving, purchased through a gift from Stephen and Bonnie Simon and the Esther Simon Charitable Trust; PR.988.26

"speaking" statue called *Pasquino* and its less loquacious partner on the Capitoline, *Marforio*, were only the most famous—had remained visible throughout the Middle Ages, serving to remind visitors and inhabitants of the city's antiquity. To some, the remains at the heart of Christendom, the seat of St. Peter and the traditional home of the papal court, might appear dangerous and "contagious," possibly spreading the plague of paganism. Nonetheless, by the fourteenth century, European visitors to the Eternal City tended not to express the fear and horror imagined by Pater; the buildings and sculptures of ancient Rome were, to the contrary, integrated into an urban image that mingled pagan and Christian creatively, producing a complex symbolic topography marked by legend.

RUINS AND MARVELS

The Rome that a curious pilgrim of the second half of the fourteenth century would have experienced was neither the magnificent Rome of antiquity nor the metropolis of today. The city was a wreck; writing in the fourteenth century, Giovanni Boccaccio (1313–1375) described it as a shipwreck and, a century later, Poggio Bracciolini (1380–1449)—anticipating Pater's rather gruesome analogy—figured the city as stripped of all beauty, prostrate like a giant decaying corpse.[2] Not only was Rome a place to see ruins, it was itself a great ruin. The roughly 25,000 inhabitants of the city—ravaged by the Black Death of the 1340s and by the recurrence of this plague for which the city was infamous—clustered around the river Tiber; the renowned seven hills were largely uninhabitable, because the astounding aqueducts that supplied them with water had, since late antiquity, fallen into disrepair. Medieval Romans rattled around the enormous enclosure provided by the Aurelian walls, built to protect and define the enormous antique city of over a million inhabitants. Within these walls, large swathes of open land—the so-called *disabitata*, the "uninhabited"—were used, primarily, as grazing grounds, or avoided for fear of the brigands who roamed in this wild internal periphery. Even in the center of the city, the populous urban spaces of antiquity were empty; the Roman Forum—the focus of civic life in the antique city—was called during the late Middle Ages Campo Vaccino, "cow pasture," while the political heart of Rome, the Capitol, was referred to as Monte Caprino, "goat hill."

Against this rather desolate backdrop, the city's Christian monuments—which today appear rather austere—must have seemed jewel-like and inviting. The most famous medieval guidebook to the city, the *Mirabilia urbis Romae* ("The Marvels of Rome"), emphasized these sites, calling its readers' attention to the biblical and apocryphal Christian stories that were said to have transpired at certain places in the city and weaving into these holy narratives fabulous tales drawn from antiquity. Composed in the twelfth century and a bestseller until the fifteenth, the *Mirabilia* rendered the city as a mystical and magical place. The text indicated those loci worthy of veneration and honor, especially the repositories of Christian relics, and those places filled with memories of pagan atrocities. The English author of this tract mingled fiction rather liberally with fact, producing a strange if effective introduction to the city as the arena where Christianity overcame paganism. Using this text, our pilgrim would have left Rome armed with notions that today seem bizarre: the great baths of the city were, in the *Mirabilia*, transformed into palaces, warmed in the winter by hot water and cooled in the summer by cold; the Lateran palace—seat of the pope—became the site where the emperor Nero gave birth to a frog; and we hear a rather marvelous recounting of the "philosophers," Phideias and Praxiteles, who in their efforts to champion the truth walked naked around the city.

One mid-fourteenth-century viewer, the Tuscan poet Petrarch (1304–1374), did not simply accept the fables of the *Mirabilia*, nor did he look on the remnants of antiquity as signs of victory over an evil empire. When Petrarch wrote in 1341 to his Roman friend, the Dominican friar Giovanni Colonna (about 1290–1348), he recalled their joint excursions walking around the city examining the antique and Christian sites and demonstrated his unbridled fondness for the former:

> We used to wander together in that great city which, though it appeared empty because of its vast size, had a huge population. And we would wander not only in the city itself but around it, and at each step there was present something which would excite our tongue and mind: here was the palace of Evander, there the shrine of Carmentis, here the cave of Cacus, there the famous she-wolf and the fig tree of Rumina with the more apt surname of Romulus, there the overpass of Remus, here the circus games and the rape of the Sabines, there the marsh of Capri and the place where Romulus vanished, here the conversations of Numa and Egeria, there the battle line of the *trigemini*.[3]

Petrarch's account of Rome, in this letter and elsewhere in his writings, is marked by a sense of nostalgia for a lost past. He repeatedly bemoaned the forgetfulness and rapacity of those who inhabited the city in his day; they, according to Petrarch, were not only unaware of the great historical importance of their environment, but also too willing to destroy or deface it.

> For today who are more ignorant about Roman affairs than the Roman citizens? Sadly do I say that nowhere is Rome less known than in Rome. I do not deplore only the ignorance involved (although what is worse than ignorance?) but the disappearance and exile of many virtues. For who can doubt that Rome would rise again instantly if she began to know herself?[4]

Scholars of the time saw Petrarch's lament as a call to cultural arms. Modern historians recognize in Petrarch's work the perception of an unspannable rift separating antiquity from his own day, and thus the beginnings of a definition of the "middle" or "dark" ages. But, as Pater succinctly put it, it was precisely the cutting of all ties with antiquity that permitted a new, fresh view of the past as a subject for study, reconstruction, and emulation.

When Poggio Bracciolini, another scholar, rode around Rome with a fellow papal secretary roughly a century after Petrarch, he too would lament the poor state of the city. Nonetheless, by the 1440s, Poggio had more reason for optimism. He entitled his ruminative work *De varietate fortunae*, "On the Inconstancy of Fortune," and saw in the ruins of Rome a reminder of the fragility of success. But while the ruins he lavished attention upon recalled to his mind the greatness of antiquity, he also recognized the possibility of fulfilling Petrarch's ideal of self-knowledge and revitalization. This optimism was based on the resettlement of the papacy in Rome. In the early fourteenth century, the pope and his court had removed to Avignon and operated under the auspices of the French monarchy. Although the desire to return to Rome never died out, practical politics made it impossible. The situation worsened with the Great Schism and a proliferation of antipopes all claiming papal authority. A degree of calm was returned to the papacy at the 1417 Council of Constance, where three claimants to the Throne of St. Peter were deposed in favor of Martin V (pope 1417–31), a scion of the Colonna, a Roman aristocratic family who counted among their number Petrarch's famous correspondent. Martin returned the papacy to Rome, but persistent unrest meant that it was only under his successors that the papacy could sustain its religious and secular power in the city. Thus Poggio, who had accompanied an antipope to the Council of Constance and spent almost his entire professional life in the papal curia, had witnessed the return of the papacy to Rome. When he finally finished his treatise on fortune in 1448, he presented it to Nicholas V (pope 1447–55), a fellow scholar and a pope bent on restoring the city of Rome to some of its ancient grandeur, a project continued under his successors, especially Sixtus IV della Rovere (pope 1471–84). Thus, a pilgrim coming to Rome at the end of the fifteenth century could, while still regretting great losses, find much to admire when surveying the city's sites, both ancient and "modern."

ROME *REDUX*

The panoramic woodcut view of *Roma* commissioned by Hartmann Schedel (1440–1514) for his encyclopedic *Liber chronicarum*, first published in Nuremberg in 1493, helps us to imagine what such a spectator would have seen (Figures 1a–b). The right side of the print places us to the northeast of the city, gazing over the Aurelian wall into the heart of Rome. Emphasis falls on this portion of the illustration, on the Borgo Vaticano and particularly on the Vatican Palace (conveniently labeled *palatium pape*). Within this complex, we can recognize the gabled roof of Old St. Peter's, the steps leading into the piazza in front of this most important church, and the crenellated building adjacent to the ancient basilica, the Sistine Chapel. This—for the time—enormous building was constructed, as its name reminds us, under Pope Sixtus IV. This pope also funded the construction of the massive Hospital of Santo Spirito, whose courtyard and church appear in the middle on the left side of the sheet, on the banks of the Tiber (Figure 1a). To its right, we can find some Roman remains: the now destroyed Meta Romuli—the odd pyramidal construction, thought by some medieval and Renaissance antiquarians, quite falsely, to contain the remains of Julius Caesar (100–44 BCE)—and, further north along the banks of the Tiber, the massive Castel Sant'Angelo, familiar to ancient Romans as the Mausoleum of Hadrian. It was on this site that Pope Gregory the Great (pope 590–604), while conducting a procession to ward off the plague, witnessed a miraculous apparition of an armed angel; the plague, naturally, subsided. Some eight and a half centuries later, in the 1450s, Nicholas V oversaw the placement of a sculpted angel on the resting place of Hadrian, probably in the hopes of garnering some of the anti-plague power so effectively harnessed by his predecessor.

Wandering across the Ponte Sant'Angelo, the virtual pilgrim using Schedel's *Liber chronicarum* enters the center of *Roma antiqua*: here, although we do see

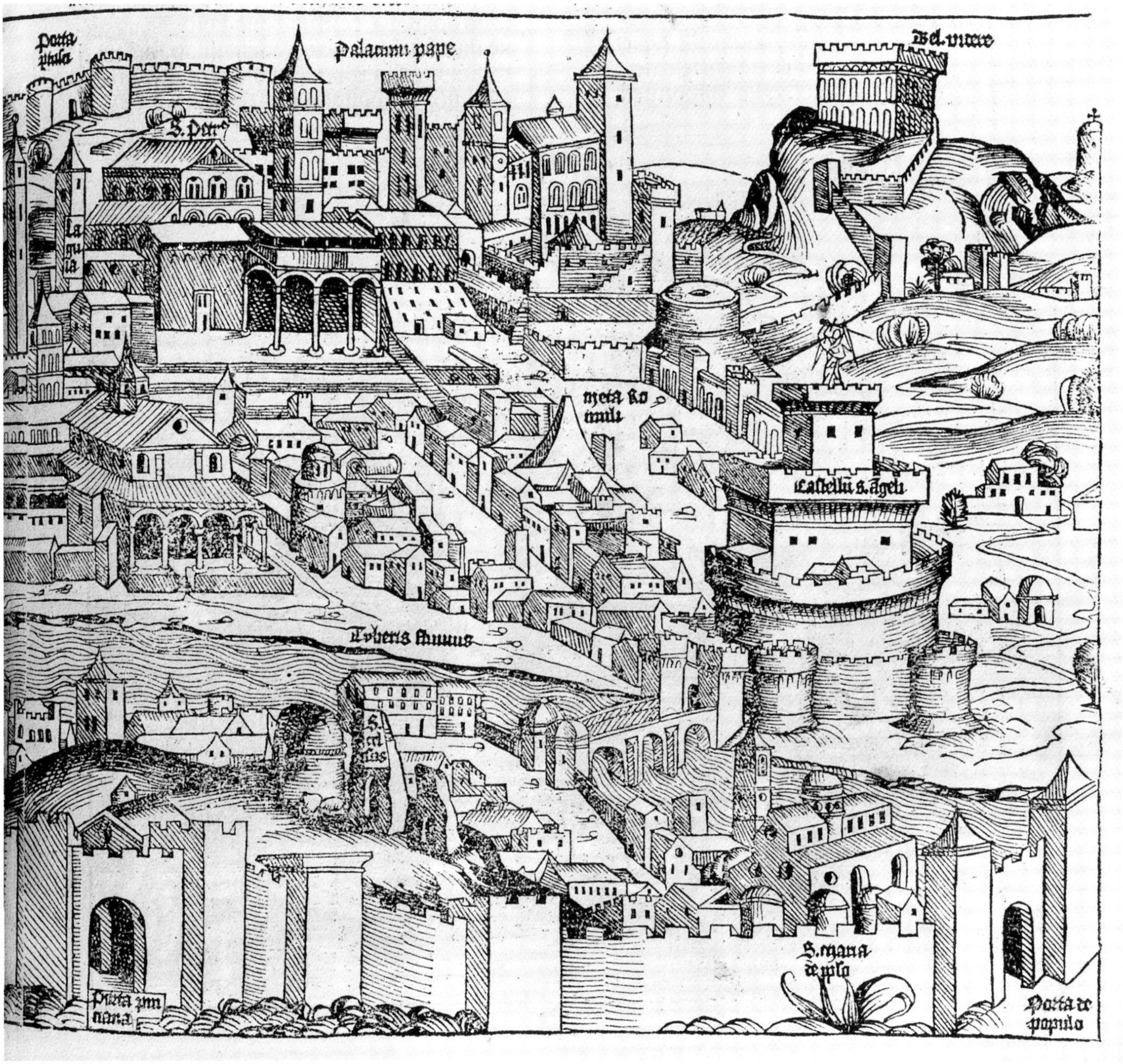

1a
Michael Wolgemut (1434/37–1519) and workshop, *View of Rome*, woodcut, in Hartmann Schedel, *Nuremberg Chronicle (Liber chronicarum)* (Nuremberg, 1493), fol. 58r, collection of Dartmouth College Library

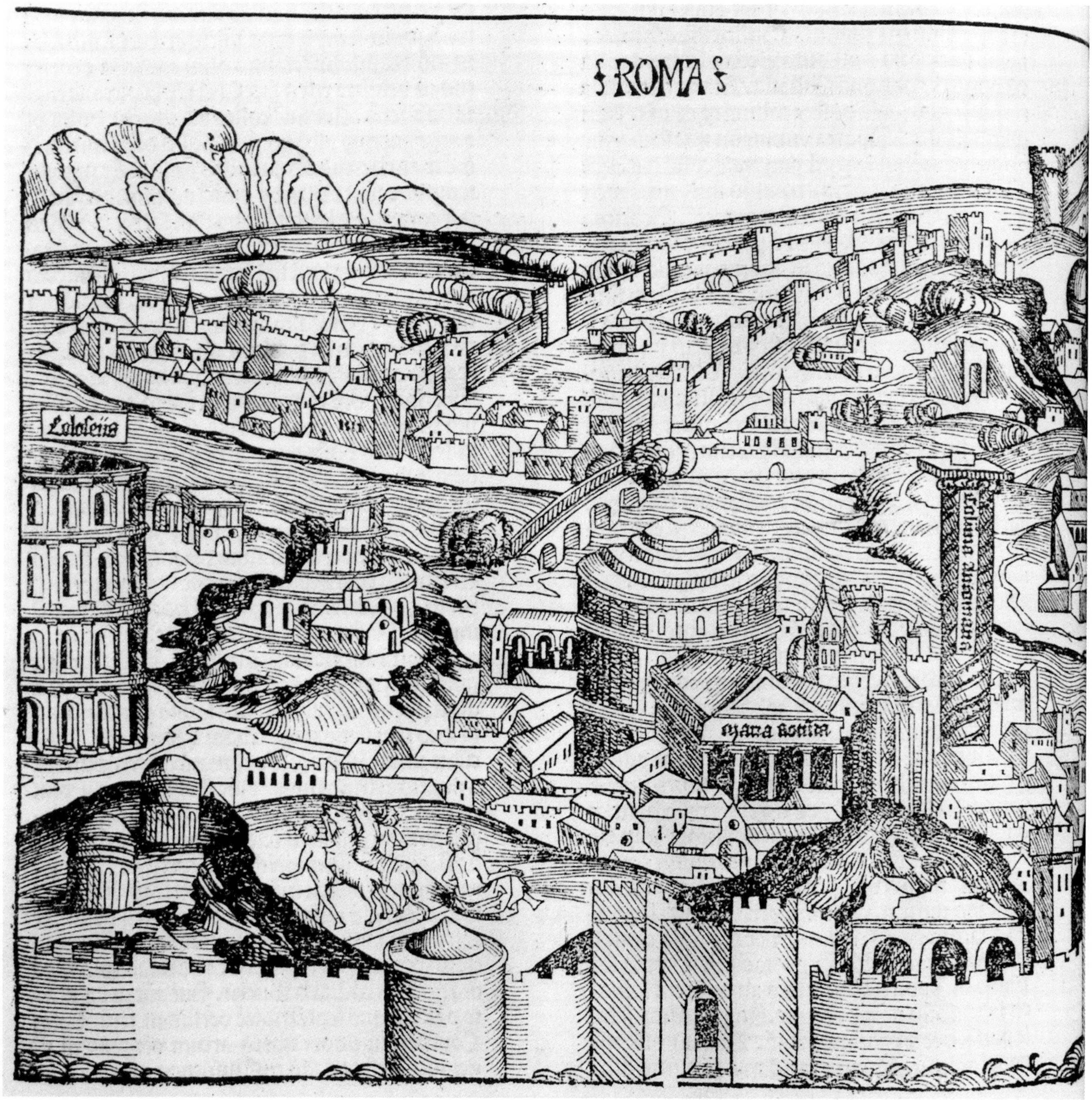

1b
Michael Wolgemut (1434/37–1519) and workshop, *View of Rome*, woodcut, in Hartmann Schedel, *Nuremberg Chronicle (Liber chronicarum)* (Nuremberg, 1493), fol. 57v, collection of Dartmouth College Library

churches—like Santa Maria del Popolo, nestled in the lower right corner—far more obvious are the remains of antiquity, some in ruins, but most well-preserved remnants of Roman glory (Figure 1b): we note the massive Antonine column, its prominence secured by an exaggeration of girth and the flamboyance of its spiraling decoration. Similarly blown into proportion with its status is the Pantheon, the scale of which rivals, in this representation, both the Castel Sant'Angelo and the Colosseum. Twisted toward us, the distinctive temple-front bears the inscription *maria rotunda*, recording its Christianized dedication to the Virgin. The Capitoline hill—with little to distinguish it in this period—is elided in favor of the Quirinal, with the *Dioscuri*, which were thought then either to have been sculpted by Phideias and Praxiteles or, as recorded in the *Mirabilia*, to portray the two naturalist philosophers as they proclaimed the truth to Roman emperors. The *Dioscuri*, or "Horsetamers," now thought to represent Alexander and Bucephalus, had survived since antiquity on the Quirinal and remain there today. In Schedel's view, they charge toward the Colosseum, which must have looked rather dilapidated at the end of the fifteenth century but has been reconstructed in the woodcut to represent the amphitheater in its pristine form, with its famous superimposed arcades restored. In fact, during the Middle Ages and Renaissance, the building was a quarry. Sixtus IV, who constructed so much in the Borgo Vaticano, also built a bridge—the Ponte Sisto, which appears in the middle of the left side of Schedel's view—in part with travertine stone excavated from the Colosseum.

Indeed, one of the central paradoxes of the Renaissance is its ambivalent relationship to ruins, on the one hand studied and revered and on the other destroyed in the search for building materials with which to reconstruct the city and so fulfill the desire to emulate antiquity. As buildings and statues were consigned to the lime kilns or pressed into service as building blocks or masonry rubble, scholars enthusiastic for antique culture—called "humanists"—sought to produce reconstructions of the city. The polymath architect Leon Battista Alberti (about 1404–1472) composed a treatise setting forth the means of producing a measured map of the city in his *Descriptio urbis Romae*; he also set about conducting some of the first truly archeological investigations, seeking to raise an antique ship from the bottom of Lake Nemi, south of Rome. But it was Alberti's humanist colleague in the papal chancery, Flavio Biondo of Forlì (1392–1463), who truly revolutionized approaches to antiquity. In his monumental treatises, *Roma instaurata* ("Rome Reconstructed," 1444–63) and *Roma triumphans* ("Rome Triumphant," 1456–60), Biondo not only engaged in an archeologically sensitive description of the physical development of ancient Rome but also examined its religious and political practices and institutions.

Despite Christianity's fundamental distrust of paganism, it was under the popes that humanist thinkers like Poggio, Alberti, and Biondo engaged in the most telling and probing analyses of antiquity, initiating an impulse that would lead to the development of a full-blown antiquarianism in the sixteenth century and, in the seventeenth and eighteenth centuries, the emergence of the discipline of archeology. That the Vatican would host the growth of such thinking is somewhat odd, and there were some moments of unease. Under Paul II (pope 1464–71), himself a great collector of antiquities, especially carved gems, humanist papal secretaries like Bartolomeo Sacchi (1421–1481), known by his *all'antica* name Platina, and Pomponeo Leto (1428–1498) were imprisoned, suspected of fomenting antipapal sentiments. It is no accident that both were impassioned lovers of the antique. Platina hunted and recorded ancient inscriptions avidly, and Leto founded and led the "Roman Academy," a club of enthusiasts who, dressing in togas and speaking Latin, congregated in the catacombs and re-enacted ancient rituals. Although both Platina and Leto were later released, their imprisonment did send a message: interest in antiquity was not to be pursued for its sake alone; it was to be placed at the service of the papacy. It was, therefore, no accident that the major figures in the drive to explain the physical remains of ancient culture worked in the papal curia. The "reconstructions" of ancient—and, especially under the popes, imperial—Rome were not only academic exercises but expressions of the desire to resurrect Rome, to raise it to the levels of majesty it achieved in antiquity, but always under the aegis of the cross. Popes felt quite justified in appropriating the title *pontifex maximus* that Roman emperors held in their roles as high priests of the state religion. This identification between pope and Roman emperor was taken a step further when Giuliano della Rovere ascended to the throne of St. Peter and chose the name Julius II (pope 1503–13), in emulation not of his obscure papal predecessor but rather—as a celebratory medal cast later in his reign records—in imitation of Julius Caesar himself.

PICTURING ANTIQUITY

Just as popes adopted Roman imperial names and cultural forms, and similar to the manner in which builders emulated Roman structures and even integrated *spolia* into the fabric of their new constructions, sculptors and painters sought to quarry useful forms from the repository of Roman art that had survived since antiquity. Indeed, in some analyses of Renaissance art, notably those of Erwin Panofsky (1892–1968), it is precisely the appearance of ancient subject matter reunited with ancient visual forms that signals the development of a new style and even the novel cultural enterprise we call "The Renaissance." There is no doubt that artists of the fifteenth century found stimulation in antique subjects and artistic forms. Their patrons too were demanding this. Humanist culture touched all areas of Italian culture during the fifteenth and sixteenth centuries, and the demand for art reflected this change.

Before 1450, the production of art was overwhelmingly Christian; art was, for the most part, commissioned for churches and sought to represent Christian figures and stories. The waxing interest in antiquity, however, brought about some startling changes. A new class of patrons, largely educated by humanists, cherished antique allusions and even began commissioning art representing ancient subjects. In so doing, artists turned quite naturally to the ruins of antiquity. Architects, painters, and sculptors, along with humanists, became the leading experts in understanding and explicating the physical remains of ancient cultures. Thus, it is hardly surprising that the artist Andrea Mantegna (1431–1506) accompanied Felice Feliciano (1433–about 1479) and some humanist friends on a famous boat trip on Lake Garda in 1464. The group deciphered Roman inscriptions and recounted the stories that took place at fabled spots on the shores of the lake. Nor is it surprising that Leo X de' Medici (pope 1513–21) would have appointed Raphael (1483–1520), a painter and architect, to oversee the antiquities in ancient Rome. It was in this context that Raphael, with the help of his humanist friend, Baldassare Castiglione (1478–1529), drew up a justly famous letter in which he outlined a preservationist approach to antique remains and demonstrated his sensitive visual response to antique sculpture. It was only Raphael's early death in 1520 that stopped the artist from carrying out Alberti's designs for a detailed map of ancient Rome. But Raphael's interests in ancient remains did find expression in his art. As with other artists, it was the manner in which Raphael responded to antiquity in his work that signaled his most profound interaction with ancient Roman culture.

The art of antiquity was known to the Renaissance in fragmentary form; of course, many antique objects—especially statues and buildings—were broken, but the available corpus of Roman art was itself partial. Renaissance artists were acutely aware of this. They lamented the almost complete lack of ancient painting, and, conversely, met every disinterred sculptural fragment with joy. In the absence of antique graphic art, it was sculpture that had the most profound effect on Renaissance art in all media. Indeed, the renowned "sculptural" quality of late-fifteenth-century painting, exemplified by the style of Mantegna, can quite convincingly be attributed to the creative manner in which Renaissance artists responded to Roman sculpture.

The fragmentariness of the Roman artistic heritage affected artists differently. Like humanists seeking to reconstruct Latin sentences confused by medieval transcriptions, many artists sought to reconstruct Roman art by filling in the blanks, some through careful study, others through rather large imaginative leaps. Artists, rather than "restoring" antiquity in their work, might instead seek historical specificity and/or a form of symbolic depth by assimilating ancient details. In the exhibition *Antiquity in Rome from the Renaissance to the Age of Enlightenment*, we find a number of examples of these approaches to antiquity.

RENAISSANCE MYTHOLOGY

Twentieth-century scholarship, responding to the rather exuberant claims of the preceding century, has taken great pains to remind us that the pagan gods did "survive," albeit transformed, throughout the Middle Ages. It is clear that during the Renaissance, however, these mythological characters again took on some of the appearance and meaning that they possessed in antiquity. This can be witnessed in a print of Hercules' struggle with the Nemean lion, reflecting an original design by Raphael (Figure 2). In representing such scenes, Renaissance artists drew inspiration from particular ancient representations of the same scene. In this work, Raphael and Vicentino emulated an antique engraved gem, and in doing so also recalled one of the most important fragments of classical statuary known during the Renaissance, the so-called *Belvedere Torso* (Figure 3), a Roman marble copy of an original Hellenistic bronze, perhaps representing Marsyas but considered then to figure Hercules.

Since this sculptural fragment had been found—possibly in the garden of Prospero Colonna (active 1430–63), Martin V's nephew—in the first half of the fifteenth century, it had become an icon of antique art, its heroic musculature and formidable dimensions speaking of power, struggle, and monumentality. Hercules was to be a favorite in the Renaissance, his heroic feats serving as an

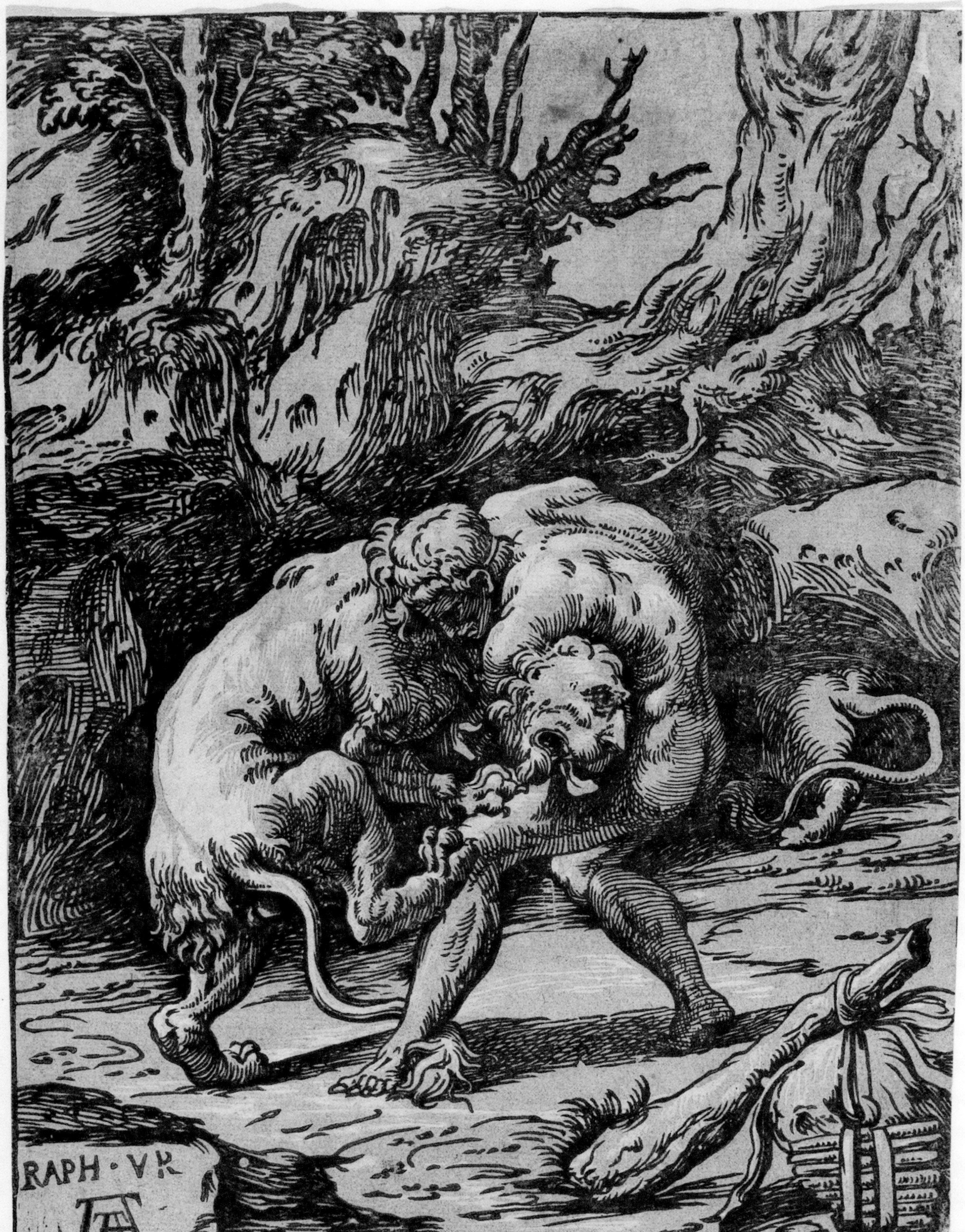
RAPH · VR

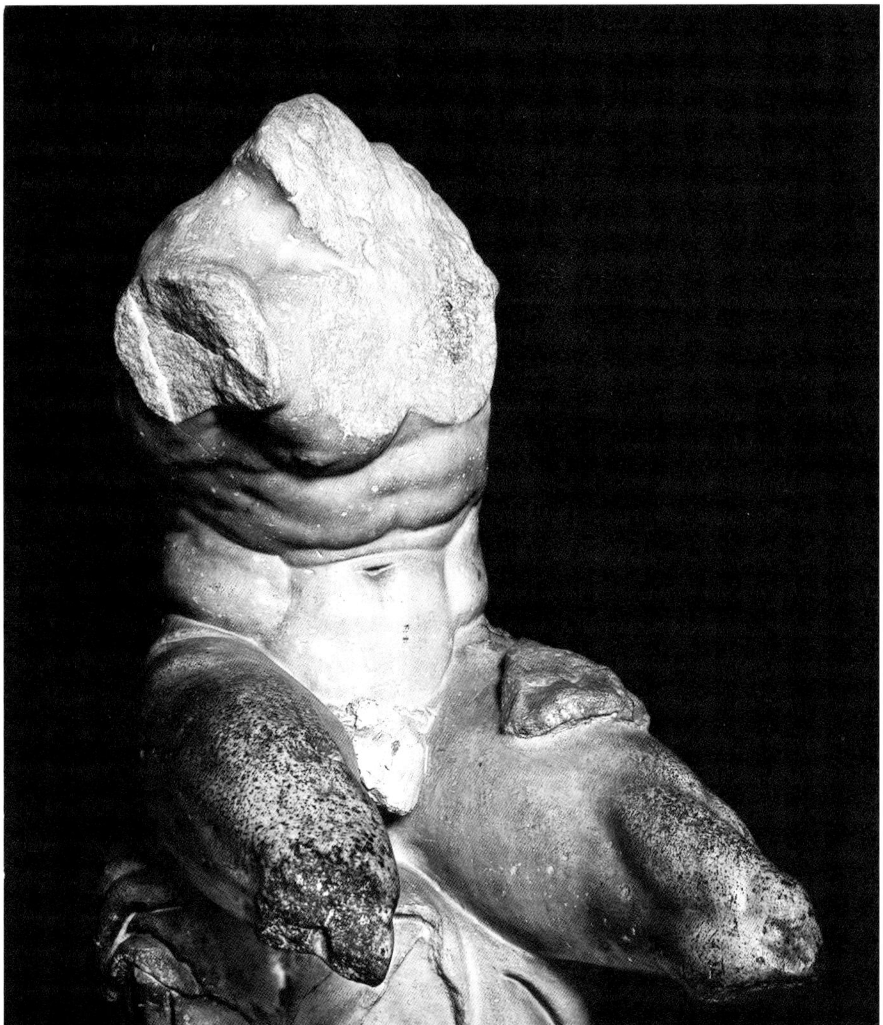

2
Andrea Andreani (1558/59–1629), after Giuseppe Nicolò Rossigliani, called Vicentino (active first half of the sixteenth century), after Raphael (1483–1520), *Hercules Wrestling with the Nemean Lion*, chiaroscuro woodcut, late sixteenth century, gift of Dr. F. H. Hirschland; PR.948.66

3
Apollonios of Athens (probably active in the first century BCE), *Belvedere Torso* (front view), marble, first century BCE, Vatican Museums, Vatican State (Alinari/Art Resource, N.Y.)

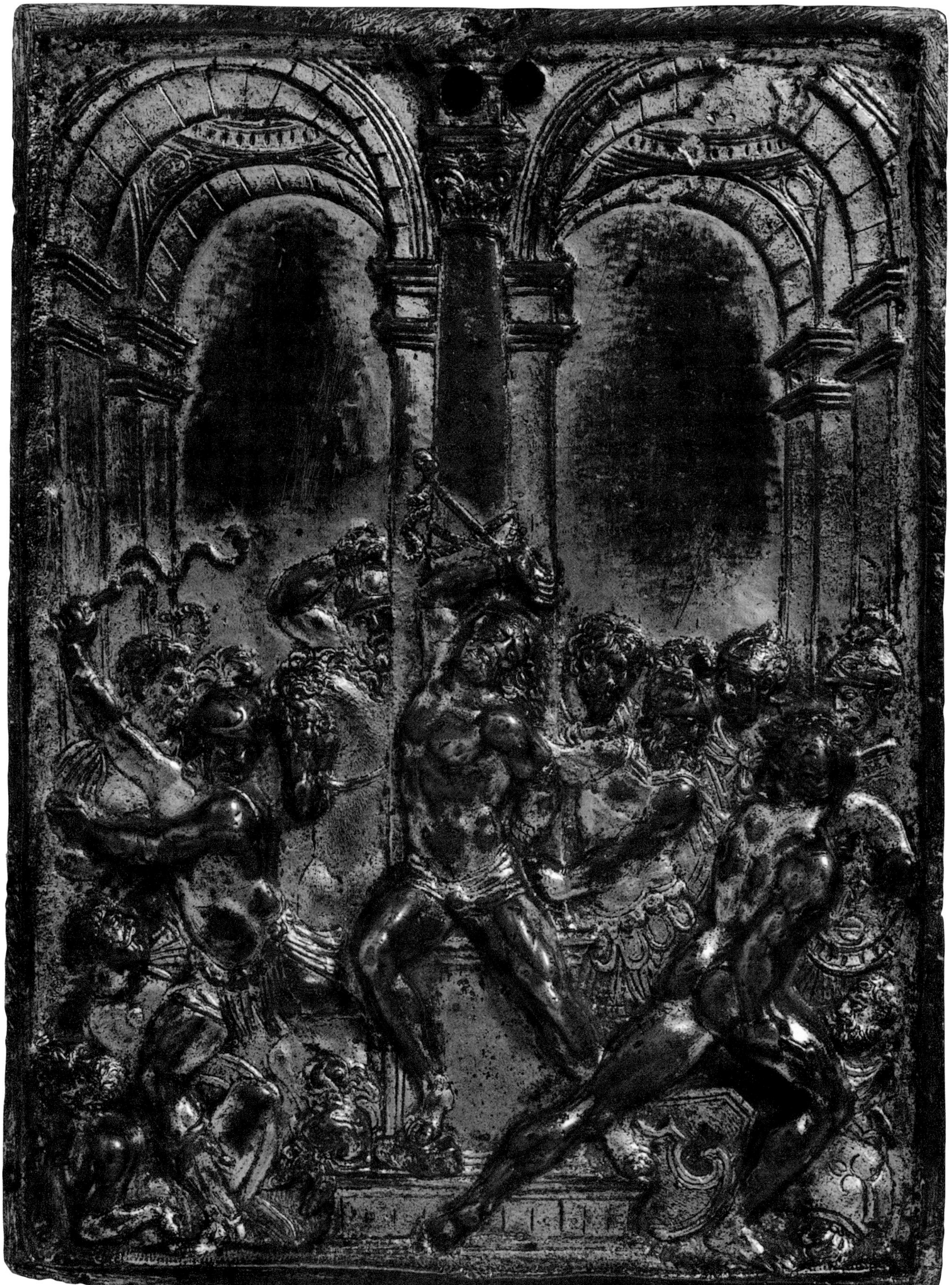

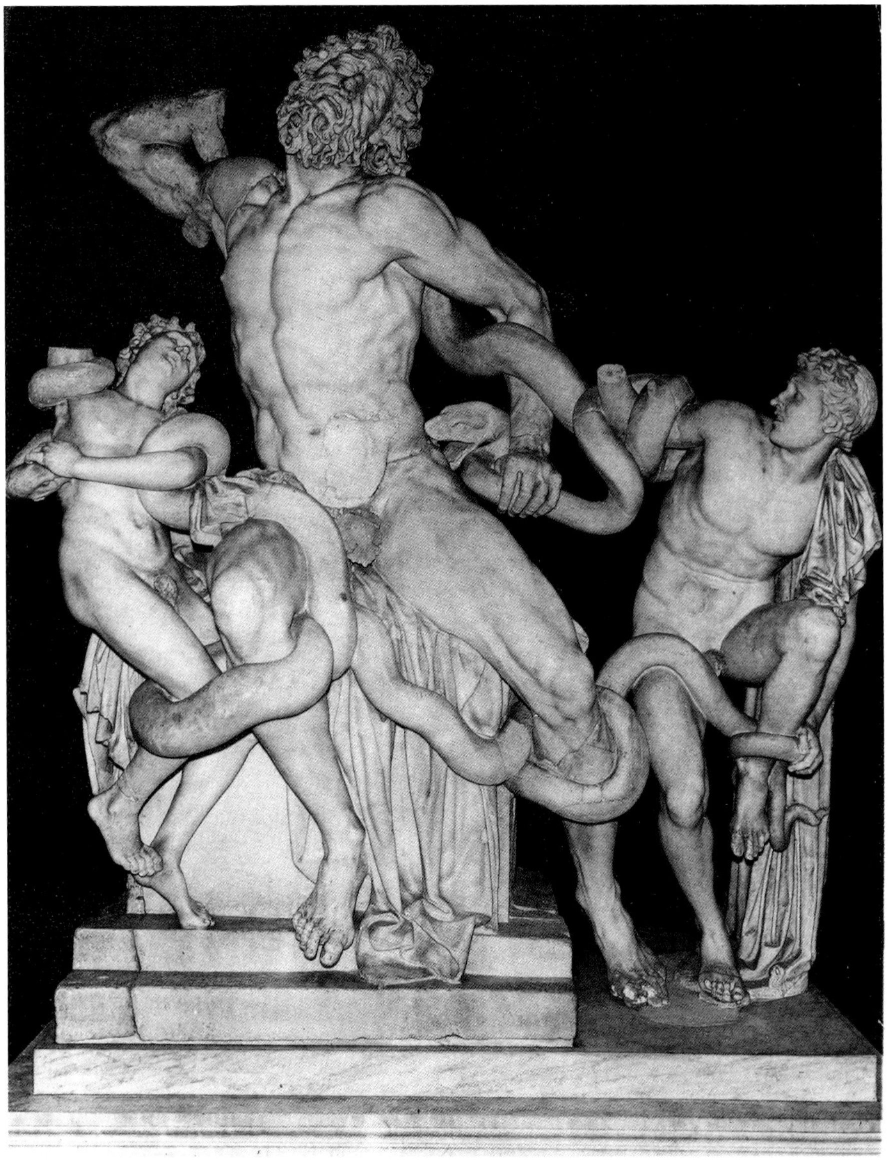

4
Galeazzo Mondella, called il Moderno (1467–1528), *The Flagellation of Christ*, gilt bronze, about 1506–09, collection of Roger Arvid Anderson, Class of 1968; EL.S.995.56.2

5
Hagesandros, Polydoros, and Athenodoros of Rhodes (active around 10–20 CE), *Laocoön* (present state, former restorations removed), marble, early first century CE, Vatican Museums, Vatican State (Giraudon/Art Resource, N.Y.)

ideal of secular mortal triumph and his supposedly asexual athletic nudity rendered unthreatening to Christian morals (indeed, Hercules was assimilated into Christian iconography as a symbol of fortitude already in the thirteenth century). Renaissance artists turning to the *Belvedere Torso* and, later, to recuperated statues like the famous *Laocoön* group, found models for dynamic and agonistic figural expression in antiquity. The antique gods of the Renaissance are, in this sense, quite different from those discovered by neoclassicists of the nineteenth century. At that time, in the wake of the antiquarian writing of Johann Joachim Winckelmann (1717–1768), artists sought in the antique a "noble simplicity and quiet grandeur." This repose was associated with classical Greek sculpture, but it does not describe the Hellenistic variants that were, for the most part, copied by the Romans and, in turn, by Renaissance artists. Instead of the calm that neoclassicists associate with antique art, Renaissance artists found a repository of meaningful gestures and strong visual tropes.

It is in this spirit that Galeazzo Mondella, called il Moderno (1467–1528), emphasized the pathos of the protagonist on his small bronze relief of the *Flagellation of Christ*, by adapting the pose of the main figure of the *Laocoön* (Figures 4 and 5); as the heroically naked priest writhes against the powerful embrace of the serpents in the Hellenistic marble, Christ in Moderno's relief struggles against his bonds and in response to the blows he receives at the hands of the Roman soldiers. Although the notion of Christ resisting his fate in this manner might have troubled theologians, it proves very effective artistically. The dynamic pose not only relates corporeal tension but also, to the visually literate, bears with it some of the pathos associated with the famous Hellenistic monument.

PATHOSFORMULAE: THE POWER OF ANTIQUE FORMS

Aby Warburg (1866–1929), writing during the first half of the twentieth century, called such poses *Pathosformulae*, or "formulas of pathos," seeing them as visual signs charged with special emotion and bearing the tradition of antique art into the modern period. Warburg's thinking is particularly important, since he reminds us of the elemental agon that attracted Renaissance artists to the antique, the polarity that he, following Friedrich Nietzsche (1844–1900), denoted as the dialectic between Apollonian and Dionysian tendencies. The former represented the struggle between the civilized, calm, and grand culture we associate with the god of the arts, Apollo, while the latter, opposed tendency signaled for Warburg the frenzied, debauched, and uncivil culture of Dionysius, the ancient god of wine and revelry. Before this struggle was repressed in the later sixteenth century, it dominated and marked the reception of antiquity in the visual arts of the Renaissance.

No better example of this exists than Mantegna's rightly famous engraving *Battle of the Sea Gods*. This large print was composed on two plates and printed on two sheets of paper, which collectors and enthusiasts could paste together in order to reproduce the visual latitude of ancient sarcophagi; the left portion of the print appears in this exhibition (Figure 6). The engraving is dominated by the active, powerfully dynamic vision of antiquity emphasized by Warburg. In the foreground,

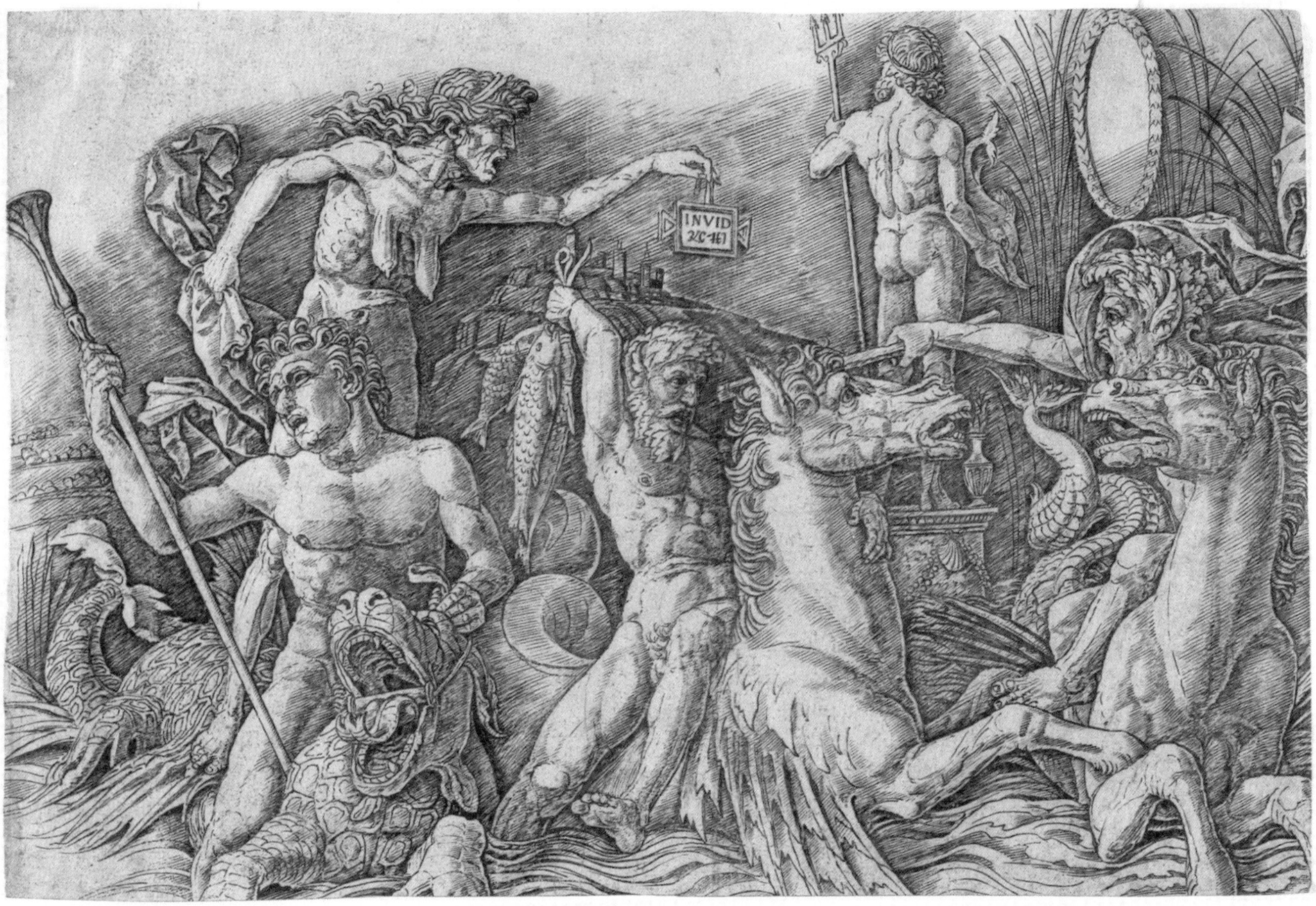

6

Andrea Mantegna (about 1431–1506), *Battle of the Sea Gods* (left half), engraving, 1470s, gift of Jean K. Weil in memory of Adolph Weil Jr., Class of 1935; PR.997.5.85

three male figures, two riding hippocamps and one mounted on what might be called a "sea dragon," twist on a roiling surf. An idealized figure to the left recalls ancient statuary; his upper body displays some of the grace we associate with the *contrapposto* pose. But his companions to the right seem to engage in vigorous battle. The leafy-eared, screaming aggressor pokes his bearded, side-saddled opponent, who, rather oddly, threatens to riposte by bringing a clutch of fish down upon his assailant's head. Behind the mock battle rises a female figure with pendulous, scrawny breasts, carrying a sign on which we recognize the word INVID, standing for *invidia*, or "envy." This emotion, we are left to conclude, somehow motivates the contest taking place before her and continuing on the right leaf of the engraving. The figures thus far described do not directly imitate antique examples, but all—especially in their nudity, their drama, and their sculptural poses—evoke antiquity directly; what is more, the image of hybrid monsters and personifications interacting in an oceanic environment calls to mind antique sarcophagi (see Figure 17). But nowhere in the print is the presence of antiquity so clearly marked as in the naked dolphin- and triton-bearing male figure with his back toward us in the background. Those attuned to the iconography of antiquity have no trouble recognizing Poseidon, or, as the Romans called him, Neptune. But this "god" does not preside over the battle, nor does he favor one side or the other with his attention. To the contrary, he is turned away from the action. This is not, moreover, Neptune himself; instead, since Mantegna sets the figure on a shell- and swag-decorated base, we see a statue of the god. The artist does not, however, refer to a well-known antique work. Instead, he fabricates an ancient statue by emulating the general appearance of Roman art; the muscular back, the evident *contrapposto*, and the pagan attributes infuse this represented statuary with what Renaissance Italians called *antichità*, a quality of "ancientness." Mantegna juxtaposes the calm repose of this figure with the wild frenzy we witness in the foreground. We are, therefore, confronted with the dual faces of antiquity described so trenchantly by Warburg: stoic restraint and frenetic action. Drawing upon the range of emotions available in the treasury of ancient *Pathosformulae*, Mantegna constructs a visual narrative with no story but evident meaning; we can feel the import without having to decode a particular narrative. For this picture has no clear textual source. The artist, not re-presenting an existing tale, instead produces a visual field marked by *antichità*.

A similar cultural ambiance infuses a famous retelling of the fateful *Judgment of Paris* engraved by Marco Dente (about 1493–1527) after a design by Raphael (Figure 7). In this print, we see the moment that the Trojan shepherd Paris gives the apple to Venus, who is pictured with her mischievous son Cupid. Behind stands Juno with her peacock, and at the center of the print, caught in the act of disrobing, is the chaste goddess Minerva, her arms set on the ground at her side. The import of this scene would have been clear: in electing the goddess of love the most beautiful, Paris set in motion the events that would lead to the Trojan war, and, in Virgil's account, to the foundation of Rome by Paris's compatriot Aeneas.

Above the main scene, various Olympians sport in the clouds; to the right, we see lounging figures, river gods and a nymph, balancing the main dramatic action. Other unidentifiable figures on the left margin of the visual field complete the lively scene. Set in an ideal landscape, allegorical and mythological figures interact with the mortal Paris. Although some wear hats or seem partially

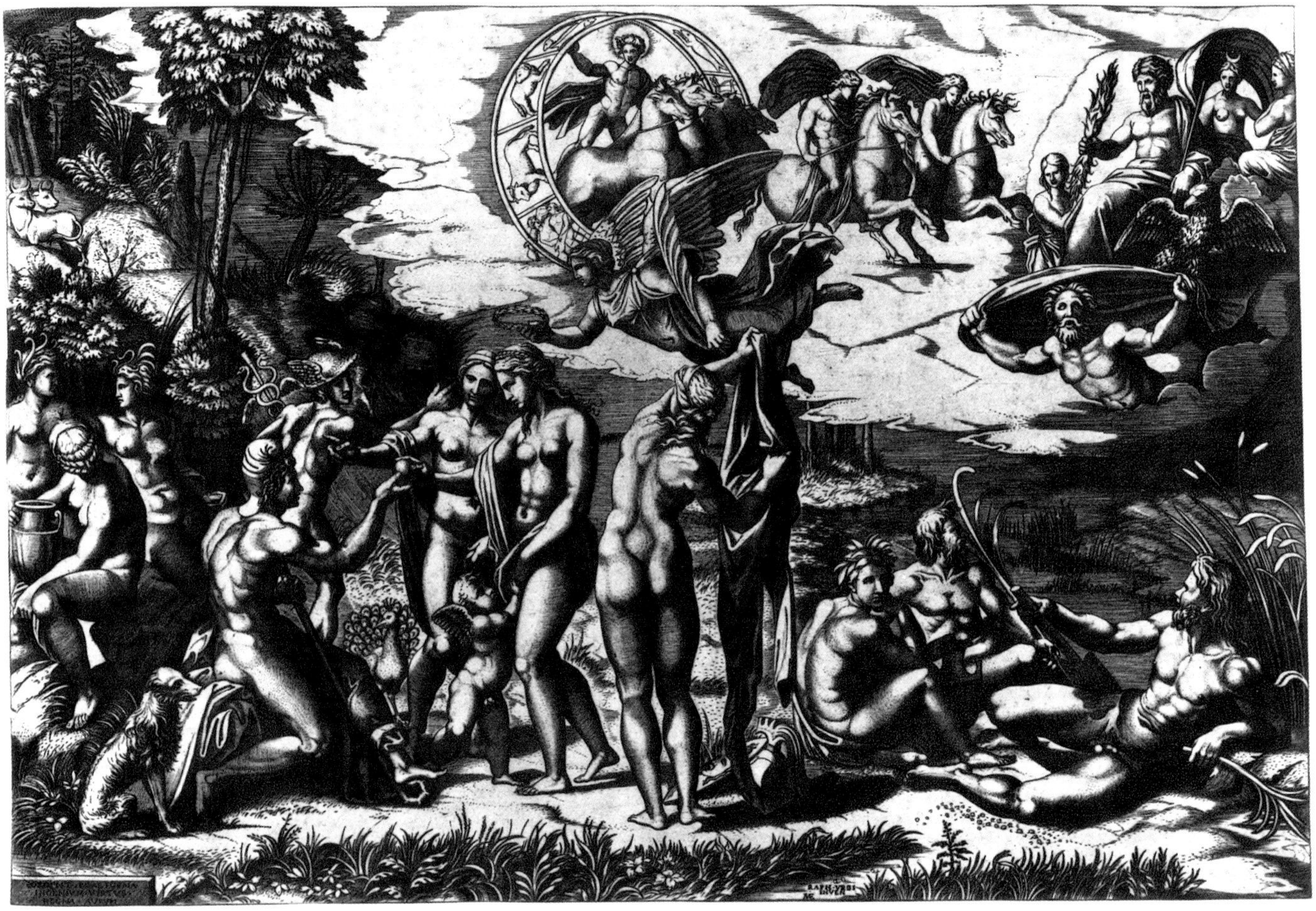

7
Marco Dente (about 1493–1527), after Marcantonio Raimondi (about 1470–about 1527), after Raphael (1483–1520), *The Judgement of Paris*, engraving, about 1520, purchased through the Julia L. Whittier Fund; PR.971.25

covered by untailored swathes of fabric, the actors here are fundamentally naked. Even Paris, who has not removed his iconographically telling Phrygian cap, has joined his fellows in removing his clothes. During the Middle Ages, unless nudity was iconographically dictated—as in the story of Adam and Eve, or the drunkenness of Noah—it was generally avoided by artists, or, if it appeared, condemned by moralists or explained away by farfetched symbolic readings. Here, heroic antique nudity seems celebrated. The lack of clothing speaks visually of Arcadia, a pagan Eden, where the trappings of civilization are rendered unnecessary by truth and by a frank understanding of the human body.

In constructing this composition, Raphael turned directly to known Roman sources. Paris's strong shoulders and back remind us again of the famed *Belvedere Torso* (Figure 3), but, in conceiving this pictorial relief, Raphael drew especially on two famous sarcophagi, one later housed in the Villa Doria Pamphili in Rome, the other in the Villa Medici. It was from the latter that the artist extracted the distinctive reclining river gods with the seated nymph, which, some three and a half centuries later, Édouard Manet (1832–1883) would put to use so effectively in his *Déjeuner sur l'herbe*. Taking advantage of his public's lack of familiarity with the more "Dionysian" aspects of ancient and Renaissance culture, Manet could scandalize French society with an iconography drawn not only from the academic paragon Raphael but also from antiquity itself. This complex interplay of motifs or "intervisuality" between different works of art and different generations of artists produces a complex web of meanings and is absolutely characteristic of Renaissance responses to antiquity. Renaissance artists did not study and record antiquity on its own terms; instead, they interpreted it, giving the bones of antiquity meaningful flesh in creative acts of reconstruction. Put differently, Renaissance artists, like the builders mining Rome for antique fragments, integrated visual *spolia* into their works.

THE SCHOOL OF ATHENS

Artists performed this integration in all media, but it was above all in engravings that artists related their synthetic antiquarianism to a broad public. The collaboration of Raphael and Marcantonio Raimondi (about 1480–1534) represents the peak of these activities. Marcantonio, a Bolognese printmaker who spent some years in Venice, found a niche in Raphael's large artistic enterprise in Rome. Although demonstrating little creative autonomy, Marcantonio did develop a technically rich means of emulating Raphael's eclectic painting style. Marcantonio's very effective manner of shading—scoring his plates with tightly ranged parallel lines—produced what is often called a "velvety" surface that does justice to the rich chromatic qualities of Raphael's work. It is perhaps for this reason that Raphael seemed so willing to work with Marcantonio and his associates. Another artist associated with this circle but not working directly under Raphael was the Mantuan engraver Giorgio Ghisi (1520–1582), whose rendition of what modern commentators call the *School of Athens* appears in this exhibition (Figure 8).

Possibly Raphael's most famous composition, this work is an icon of Renaissance syncretism: the creative joining of Christian and pagan. The fresco on which Ghisi bases his engraving was commissioned by Julius II della Rovere, the nephew

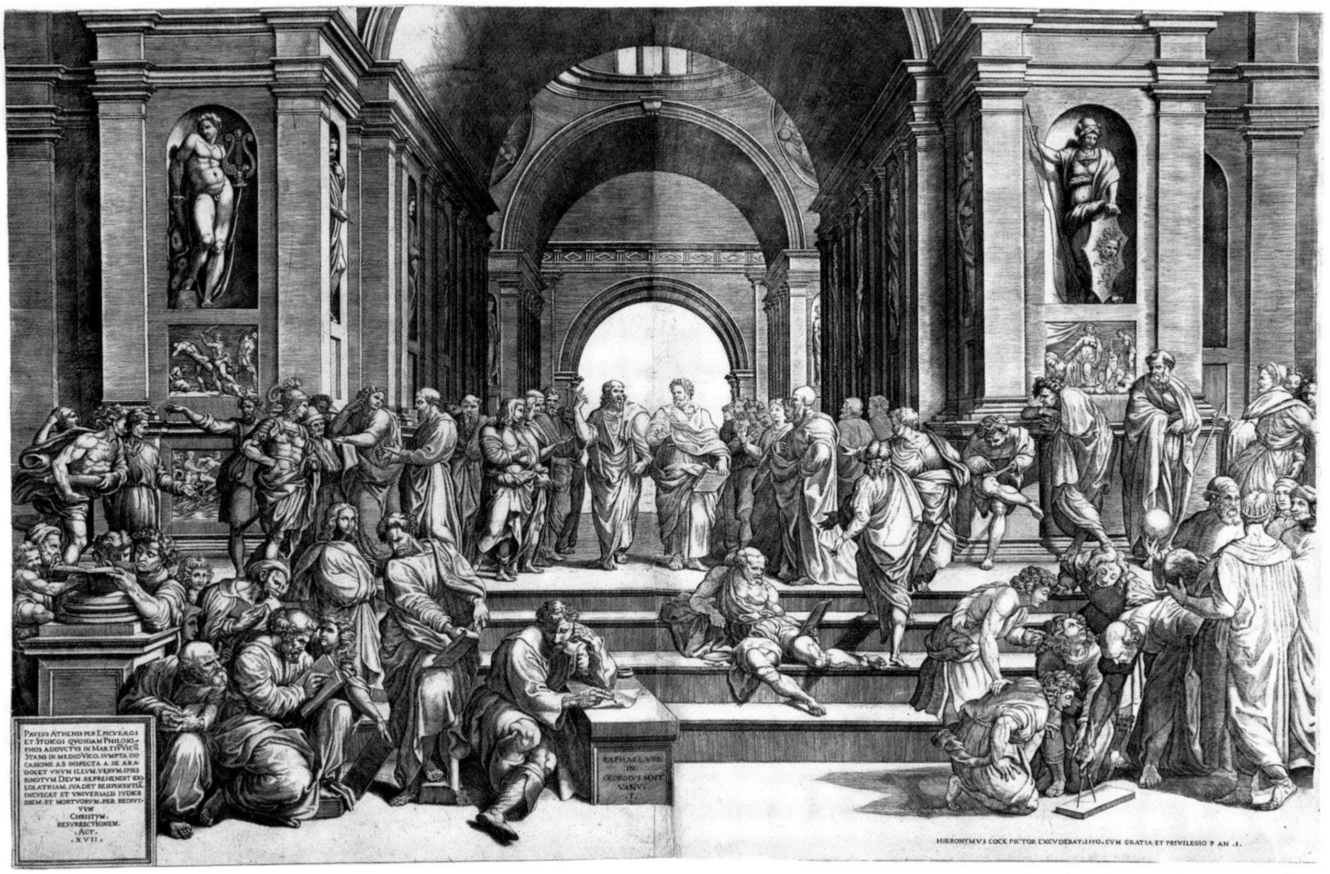

8

Giorgio Ghisi (1520–1582), after Raphael (1483–1520), *The School of Athens*, engraving, 1550, gift of Jane and W. David Dance, Class of 1940; PR.991.58.1

of Sixtus IV and patron of Michelangelo's paintings on the ceiling of the chapel built by Sixtus. Raphael's mural—a rendition of Philosophy—appeared along with other paintings illustrating the major branches of knowledge—Theology, Poetry and Jurisprudence—in Julius's private library, a room later called the Stanza della Segnatura. Within a spacious *all'antica* hall, punctuated with statuary set into niches in the walls, we witness a congregation of antiquity's greatest philosophers. At the center, the idealist Plato points up to the heavens, while his companion Aristotle, the father of the natural sciences, seems to indicate his interest in the natural world through a measured salute toward the viewer. Ranged around these two luminaries are their colleagues from various places and periods of antiquity. To the right, Diogenes, the poor, enlightened philosopher, sprawls across the steps. Further to his right, Euclid the geometer (traditionally thought to be represented in the likeness of architect Donato Bramante [about 1444–1514]) bends over to prove a point to the audience of pupils arrayed around him. To the left of center, Socrates lectures. In the left foreground, Pythagoras demonstrates his theories to a group of acolytes, while brooding in the center foreground is Heraclitus, the stoic, melancholic philosopher, whom Raphael has given—with some humor—a visage contemporaries would have understood as resembling Michelangelo (1475–1564), the moody artist slaving away on the Sistine ceiling while Raphael painted in the Stanza della Segnatura. This academic conference takes place in a distinguished building that seems to evoke a reassuring ecclesiastical ambiance while nevertheless proclaiming its pagan heritage. Statues of Apollo and Athena flank the scene, surmounting illusionistic reliefs telling tales drawn from ancient texts. The monumental architecture, although thought by some to reflect Bramante's ongoing construction of New St. Peter's, does not relate to any identifiable ancient building. It does appear, however, to be a "reconstruction": an ideal view of how antiquity, if whole, would have appeared. The fragments of ancient Rome—its broken buildings and partial sculptural bodies—are imagined as complete, producing an ideal and artificial image that has in many ways become the most powerful historical vision of antiquity. When we imagine ancient Greece, we do so through Raphael's eyes.

Curiously, however, in the painting and in Ghisi's print, this apparently integral vision of antiquity contains reminders of ruination. In the left foreground, Heraclitus/Michelangelo rests his elbow on a large chunk of marble; similarly, the philosophers to his left also strike poses using what appear to be fallen blocks of stone. The allusions to ruins in works such as this are odd. Here, the fragments might refer to the partiality, or inherent instability, of ancient—as opposed to Christian—thinking; or, perhaps more likely, they indicate a general aesthetic appreciation of the fragment and the sweet nostalgia that it evokes.

RAPHAEL'S RUINS

The symbolic profundity of the ruin becomes most clear in religious iconography. We see it, for example, in Marcantonio Raimondi's engraved version of a tapestry representing *St. Paul Preaching in Athens* (Figure 9), for which his mentor, Raphael, had provided the designs. Raphael's tapestries for the Sistine Chapel were produced in the middle of the second decade of the

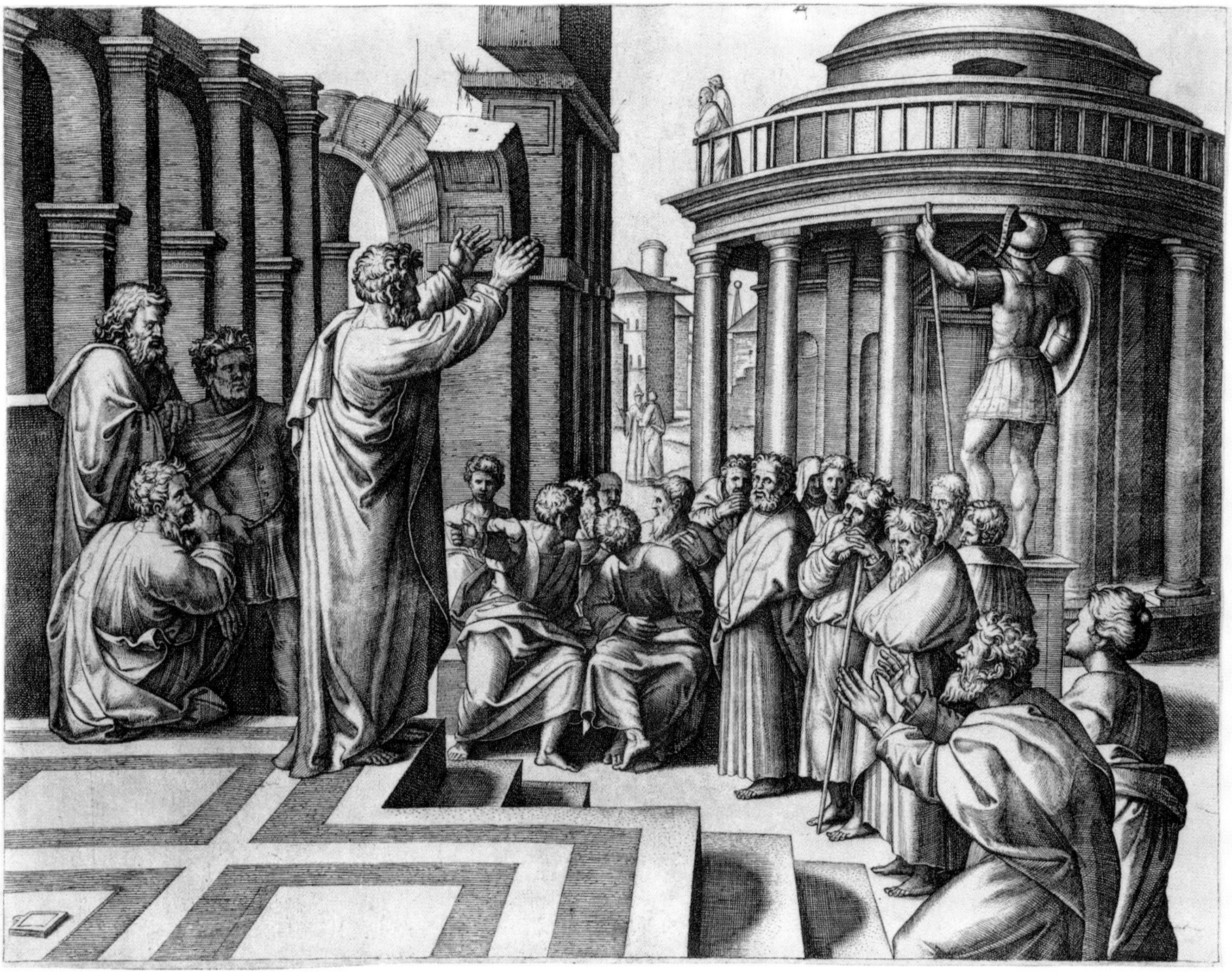

9
Marcantonio Raimondi (about 1470–about 1527), after Raphael (1483–1520), *Saint Paul Preaching in Athens*, engraving, about 1517–20, purchased through a gift from Stephen and Bonnie Simon and the Esther Simon Charitable Trust; PR.988.26

sixteenth century and were one of the most important undertakings of the artist's career. The tapestries represented scenes from the lives of Saints Peter and Paul. In copying his master's design, Marcantonio Raimondi was not "plagiarizing." Marcantonio had been accused of such practices by Albrecht Dürer (1471–1528) in the early years of the sixteenth century, resulting in a judicial proceeding that is a watershed in the history of copyright. But, working under Raphael's supervision, Marcantonio helped the Urbinate painter to circulate in print form his compositions, which would then become the basis of European academic painting until the nineteenth century.

Although the print of *St. Paul Preaching in Athens* differs from Raphael's design in certain details, it fundamentally reflects its model. Raphael seeks, in this work, to reconstruct the Athenian Areopagus, the Hill of Ares and site of the courts of justice in the ancient city. In so doing, he includes a large arcade on the left and, to the right, a round temple with Doric columns not unlike the famous Tempietto, which his countryman Bramante constructed a decade before on the Janiculum hill in Rome at the site where St. Peter was said to have been martyred. In Raphael's tapestry design, and in Marcantonio's engraving after it, St. Paul urges the Athenians to join him—a former Roman soldier—in following the precepts of Christianity. The Athenians are represented variously as caught in contemplation, on the cusp of conversion, or engaged in lively debate. Pictorially, however, they have turned their backs on the large statue of Ares, the *genius loci* of the Areopagus. Reminiscent of Mantegna's averted Neptune, Raphael's Ares turns away from the main scene. Caught in a distinctive *contrapposto* and bearing a spear, a shield, and a helmet, the pagan god of war seems to react to the powerful, hortative gesture of Paul. The effect of the saint's proselytizing on the assembled Athenians hangs in the balance, but the statue of Ares seems already "aware" of Christianity's eventual triumph. Raphael underscores this victory by including, amidst the splendid ancient architecture, the suggestion of ruin. Above Paul's head, we see the stump of an arcade, surely not a part of the Areopagus in the first century CE. Above the arcade, we even see grassy shoots sprouting from a stony architectural ledge. These proleptic allusions to ruins foreshadow the failure of paganism: like lichen on rock, Paul's words will take hold in the minds of the Athenians.

Similar tufts of grass grow in the many crevices visible in the ruins included in the background of Marcantonio's engraving after Raphael, *Holy Family with Saint John the Baptist,* sometimes—and for obvious reasons—called the *Virgin with the Long Thigh* (Figure 10). In an iconographical grouping quite common during the Renaissance, the Holy Family—Mary, Christ, and St. Joseph—is joined by the infant John the Baptist, who, prefiguring his later role as the herald of Christ, recognizes the savior; the scroll he holds usually reads *Ecce agnus Dei*, "Behold the lamb of God." In this version, another rather mysterious figure appears—a "voyeur" witnessing the scene from the middle ground but, as far as we can tell, unobserved by the protagonists. Although one would imagine that this congregation would have taken place in Bethlehem, the site of the nativity, the setting we see in the engraving does not appear to be the stable mentioned in the Evangelists' accounts. (Marcantonio does include a donkey, poking his nose into the visual field at the left, reminding us perhaps of the biblical setting.) Instead of a stable, the narrative plays out in front of an involved architectural complex. A

10
Marcantonio Raimondi (about 1470–about 1527), after Raphael (1483–1520), *Holy Family with Saint John the Baptist*, engraving, about 1520–25, purchased through a gift from Stephen and Bonnie Simon and the Esther Simon Charitable Trust; PR.988.27

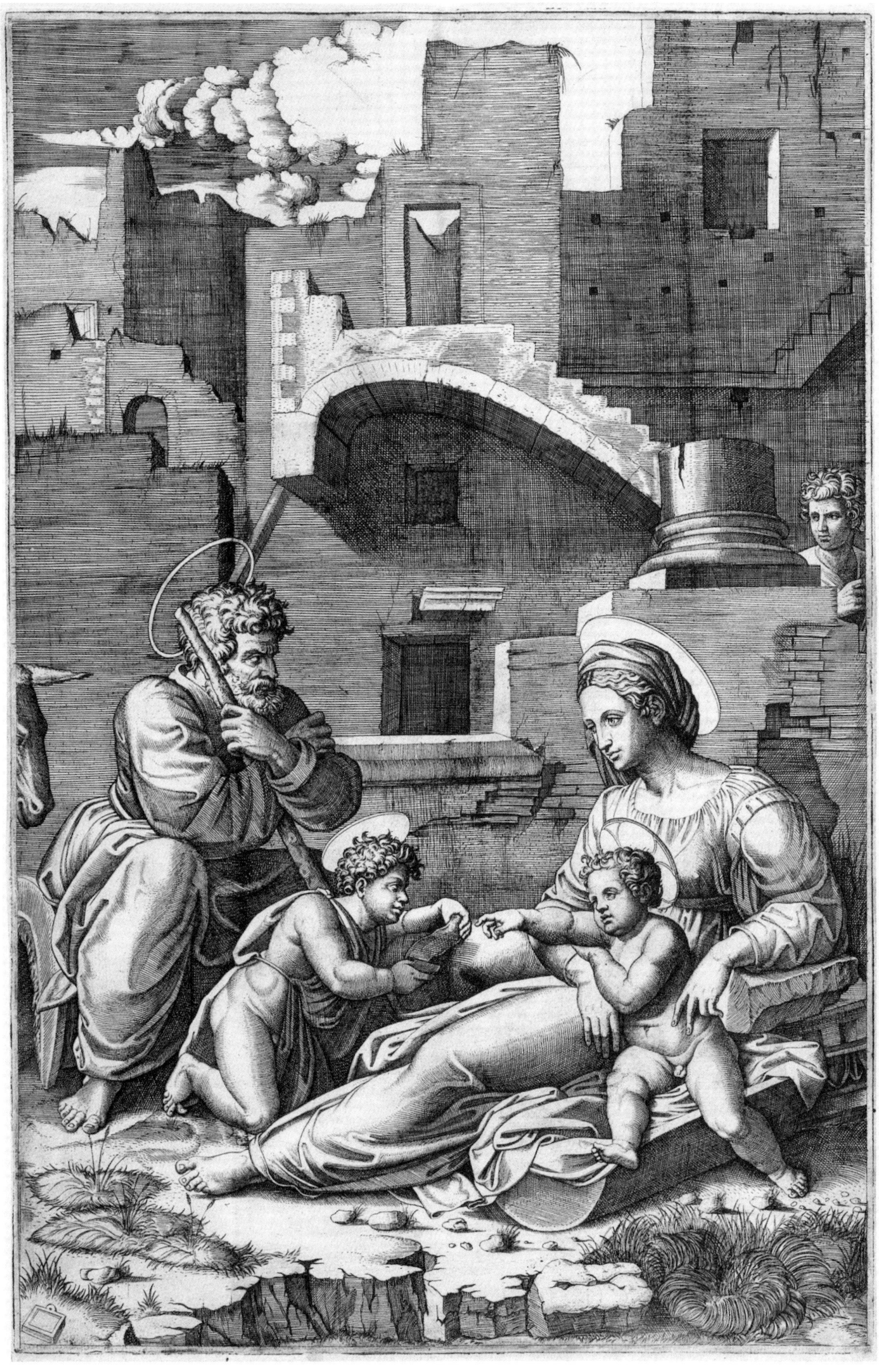

stepped wall behind Joseph and Mary rises to the cracked stump of a column. Further back looms a two-story structure punctuated by doorways and windows; access to the second story is supplied by a staircase, apparently marble, whose distinctive arch connects the two sides of the figural composition in the foreground. The background walls rise to jagged or unfinished heights; they appear to have tumbled down. The internal spaces they define seem empty and roofless, and the urban scape of the background is desolate. A particularly sensitive detail in the center of the composition shows the decorative lintel over a darkened portal; the doorway suggests the emptiness within, while the broken cornice reminds us of the inexorable entropy that has wrought such havoc on so imposing a structure.

The inclusion of these obvious ruins in the background of the sacred drama helps Raphael, and Marcantonio, to invest the Christian story with symbolic depth. Various tales informed medieval viewers of how, when a virgin bore a child, certain ancient structures would crumble. Such legends encouraged Renaissance artists to include in the background of their Nativities the suggestion of Roman ruins. The fallen stones indicated the transitory nature of pagan hegemony and the power of the new covenant under Christ. Certainly, the ruins in the *Virgin with the Long Thigh* might be seen within this iconographic tradition.

But they also function less textually, reflecting a growing sensibility that ruins could act as pathos-filled emotional markers. They seem to charge the visual field with a sense of nostalgia and profound loss. Exhibiting the type of emotion we first encountered with Petrarch's lamenting of the fallen glory of Rome, the shattered remains of ancient Rome inspire feelings not only of Christian triumph but also of regret felt with the passage of time. This aesthetics of entropy serves to invest the interplay between the actors with a psychological depth. The moment that John recognizes Christ as the savior marks Mary's prophetic understanding of her son's fate on the cross. Her voided, visionary gaze and melancholy air remind us all of what is to come. The architecture of the Holy Family too will crumble in the inexorable narrative of Christian salvation. By including atmospheric ruins, the artists invest their work with a pervasive and touching mood. But Raphael and Marcantonio used antiquity as more than an emotional resource; both Mary and the Christ child in this print are inspired by Michelangelo's vision of the *Creation of Man*, immortalized on the ceiling of the Sistine Chapel. While Mary's lounging pose and extended leg recall Adam's sprawling worldliness, Christ's extended, muscular arm unmistakably reproduces the life-giving gesture performed by God the father in Michelangelo's monumental fresco.

NOSTALGIA AND DESIRE

The appropriation of Michelangelo's forms reminds us of the synthetic qualities of Renaissance visual culture in general and of Renaissance approaches to antiquity in particular. The representation of ancient places and objects in this period was not marked by archeological specificity or antiquarian precision; instead, antiquity for Renaissance artists and viewers was a repository of powerful motifs. What is more, although humanists trained in philology sought to reconstruct from the fragmentary textual and physical remains of ancient Rome a satisfying whole, most artists and viewers were more interested in the visual power

11
Unknown, Italian (active late fifteenth century), *Elephant and Obelisk*, woodcut, in Francesco Colonna, *Hypnerotomachia Poliphili* (Venice, 1499), collection of Dartmouth College Library

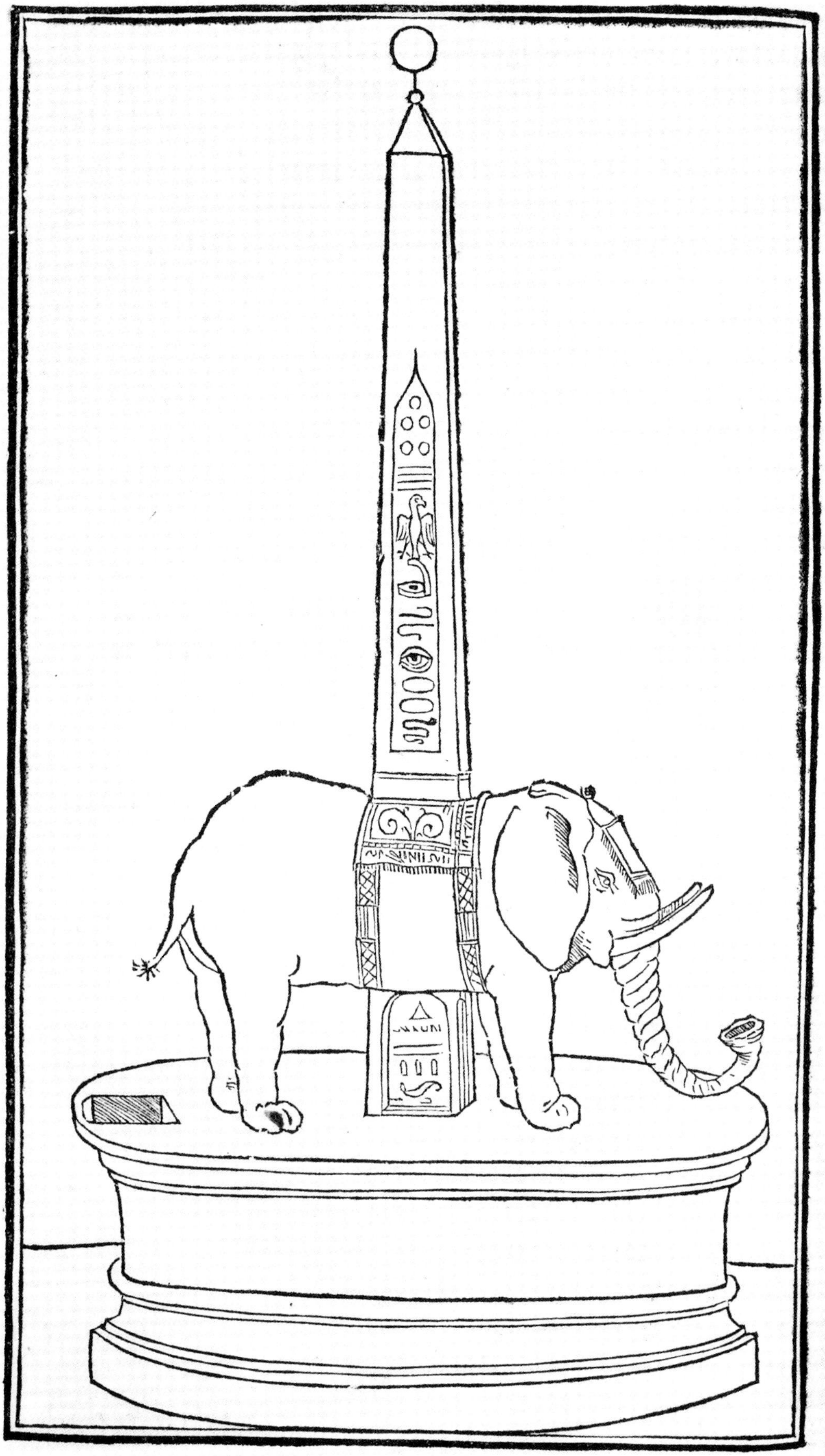

of antiquity and its complex and indecipherable mysteries for which the "ruin" stood as a concrete allegory.

Nowhere is this sensibility more clearly demonstrated than in the curious and fabulous book called the *Hypnerotomachia Poliphili*, first published at the press of Aldus Manutius (?1450–1515) in 1499, although parts of the text may have been composed earlier. The Aldine edition does not provide an author's name, but the initial letters of the chapters do form an acrostic spelling out POLIAM FRATER FRANCISCUS COLUMNA PERAMAVIT, meaning "Brother Francesco Colonna greatly loved Polia." Most assume that Francesco Colonna (1433–1527) was the author of the *Hypnerotomachia Poliphili*, which tells—as its evocative pseudo-Greek title suggests—a story of the "amorous" (*eroto*) "strife" (*machia*) of Poliphilo, who "loves much" (*poly* + *philo*) in a dream (*hypnos*). The text meanders with its dreaming protagonist through gardens and ruins, following his quest to secure the love of Polia. Along the way, Poliphilo and Polia encounter mythological deities and monumental sculpture, including, for example, the massive *Elephant and Obelisk* (Figure 11). "It was made," Poliphilo recounts, "from a rock blacker than obsidian, thickly dusted with gold scintillae and silver specks that sparkled in the stone. Its extreme hardness was shown by the bright lustre which caused objects to be reflected in it everywhere. . . ."[5] Above and below the elephant was an ancient obelisk, "made from greenish Lacedaemonian stone," "which tapered up to the pointed tip," and which had "Egyptian characters beautifully drawn on three of its faces." Such hieroglyphs, which Renaissance humanists struggled unsuccessfully to read, were nonetheless revered in antiquarian thought, regarded by Alberti as powerful symbols and thought by Ficino to represent the ideas of the gods. The accompanying woodcut illustration of this fabulous monument describes the hieroglyphs in some detail. Poliphilo finds a stairway and ascends not only onto the pedestal but also into the belly of the elephant itself. Here, within the stony beast, he finds two sarcophagus-like chests, each surmounted by a naked figure, a man and a woman. Each figure holds a shield, on which Poliphilo finds a mysterious inscription repeated in Hebrew, Greek, and Latin.

The narrative and meaning of the *Hypnerotomachia Poliphili* are as opaque as its rhetoric and illustrations are clear. The lucid vision of the monumental elephant and obelisk is oddly juxtaposed with the open-ended and puzzling inscriptions in antique languages. Tangible yet hermetic and distant, the monument seems to be an ironic allegory meditating on the hunger for a logical and monumental antique past and on that past's actual composite and baffling nature. The restored Rome of the Renaissance, the author seems to suggest, was as hollow as the elephant and as ultimately indecipherable as the hieroglyphics on the obelisk.

The *Hypnerotomachia Poliphili* reminds us that during the Renaissance a range of approaches to antiquity existed. Although the period certainly saw the flourishing of historicist, philological, and archeological analyses of the Roman past, it also retained both a strong nostalgia for ruins and a sense of wonder for the bewildering and often incomprehensible mysteries of antiquity.

Novel, however, was the intensity of the desire with which Europeans of this period turned to ancient Rome for answers to contemporary problems. Above all, it was a sense of legitimacy that Europeans sought when assembling, studying, and aping Roman culture. Reconstructing an imaginary whole from these remains formed the basis for the imitative projects we associate with the Renaissance.

Simultaneously, lamenting the irretrievable loss of antique culture emerged as a ritual of identification: to mourn the passing of Rome was to claim an intimate relation to the deceased. In the humanist's oft-repeated lament *quanta Roma fuit ipsa ruina docet,* one recognizes the plaintive longing for past glory, but one also senses pride. In studying, describing, and seeking out ruins, Europeans sought ancestors. It was this insatiable genealogical desire that drove Renaissance individuals to collect and value Roman material culture and led Renaissance artists to emulate, iconographically and formally, the art of antiquity.

Notes

1. Walter Pater, "Winckelmann," in *Selected Works*, ed. Richard Aldington (New York: Duell, Sloan, and Pearce, 1948), 121.

2. Poggio Bracciolini, *De varietate fortunae* (Paris: D. Gregorius, 1723; reprinted Bologna: Forni, 1969), 5–7.

3. Francesco Petrarch, *Rerum familiarium libri I–VIII*, trans. Aldo S. Bernardo (Albany, N.Y.: State University of New York Press, 1975), 291.

4. *Ibid.*, 293.

5. *Hypnerotomachia Poliphili: The Strife of Love in a Dream*, trans. Joscelyn Godwin (London: Thames and Hudson, 1999), 36.

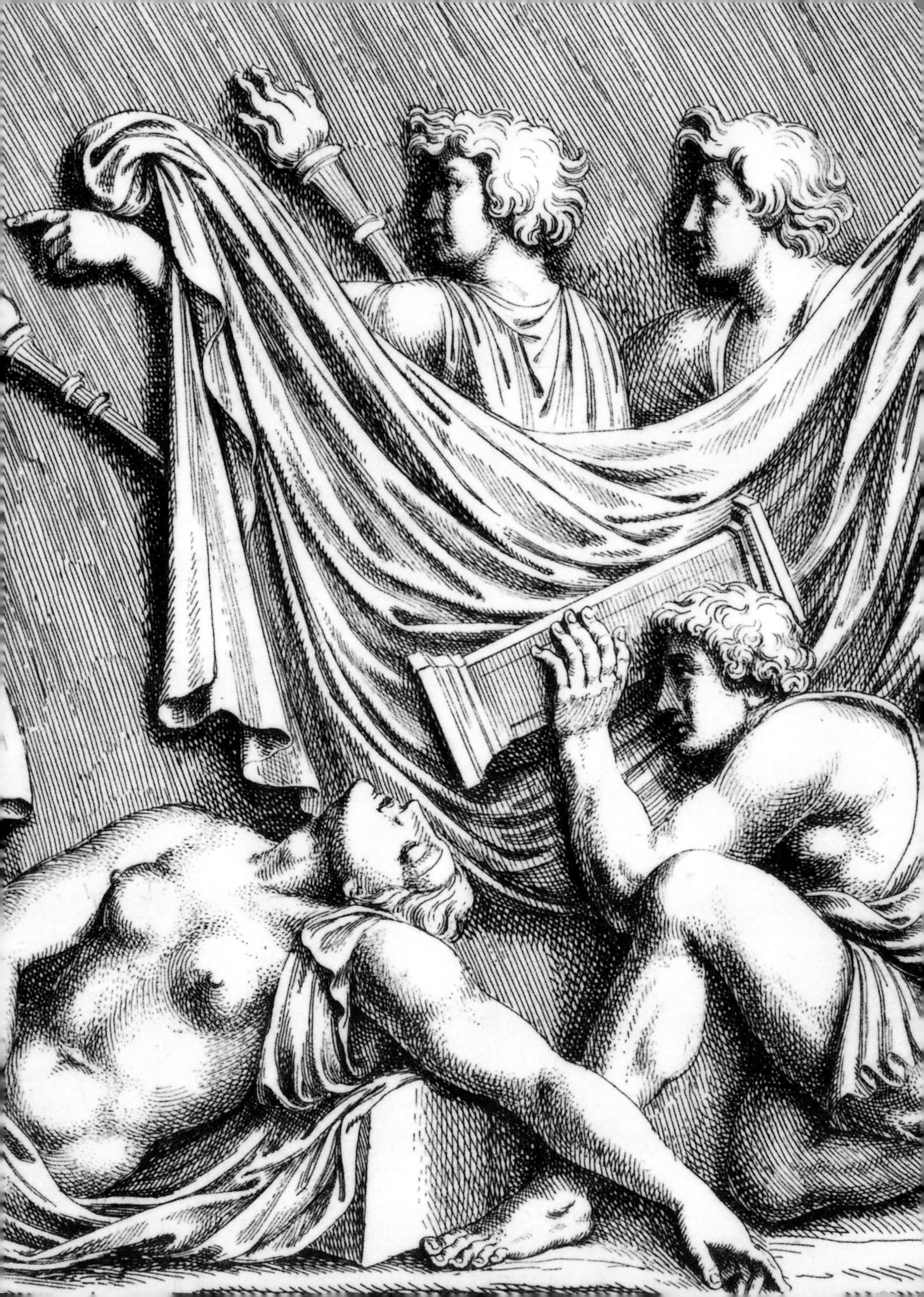

Survival and Revival of the Classical Tradition: Antiquity in Rome from the Baroque Era to the Age of Enlightenment

T. Barton Thurber

> From the vast and venerable [remains of antiquity] is risen like a phoenix from its ashes this newfangled Rome. . . . Yet, whoever carefully considers all the evidence will ultimately realize that ruined Rome crumbling under the weight of innumerable centuries remains almost like an ancient mother . . . , [whose] grand style is always to be imitated and is always inspiring. (Angelo Grillo, 1590) [1]

The Benedictine abbot Angelo Grillo (1557–1629) poetically described the dramatic changes that had occurred in Rome during the reign of Pope Sixtus V (1585–90), during which time the city began its evolution toward becoming a modern capital. In addition to the construction of innovative buildings, streets, and squares that marked the creation of a new Rome, however, Grillo also stressed the harmonious relationship between the ancient past and recent events. Indeed, in his opinion, it seemed as though the dispersed remains of antiquity were reunited in order to form a new classical tradition. This trend was supported by the continued study of surviving texts and artifacts, combining a mixture of serious methodology and romantic enthusiasm. Moreover, as foreign personages and professionals admired the magnificence of Roman civilization, local princes and patricians competed with one another to adorn their residences with newly discovered sculptures, forming sizable collections of antiquities. At the same time, antique monuments were studied by nearly every promising painter, sculptor, and architect. Their impressions led to fantastic reconstructions and inspired them to recreate and even to surpass the splendors of the past. The resulting idealized image of Rome had as powerful an impact as the real city on art and architecture throughout Italy and the rest of Europe for hundreds of years.

OPPOSITE:
Pietro Santi Bartoli, 1635–1700, after unknown, Roman, active second century CE, *Roman Sarcophagus Representing Orestes' Revenge* (detail), engraving, in *Admiranda romanarum antiquitatum . . .* (Rome: Domenicus de Rubeis, 1693), plate 52, collection of Dartmouth College Library

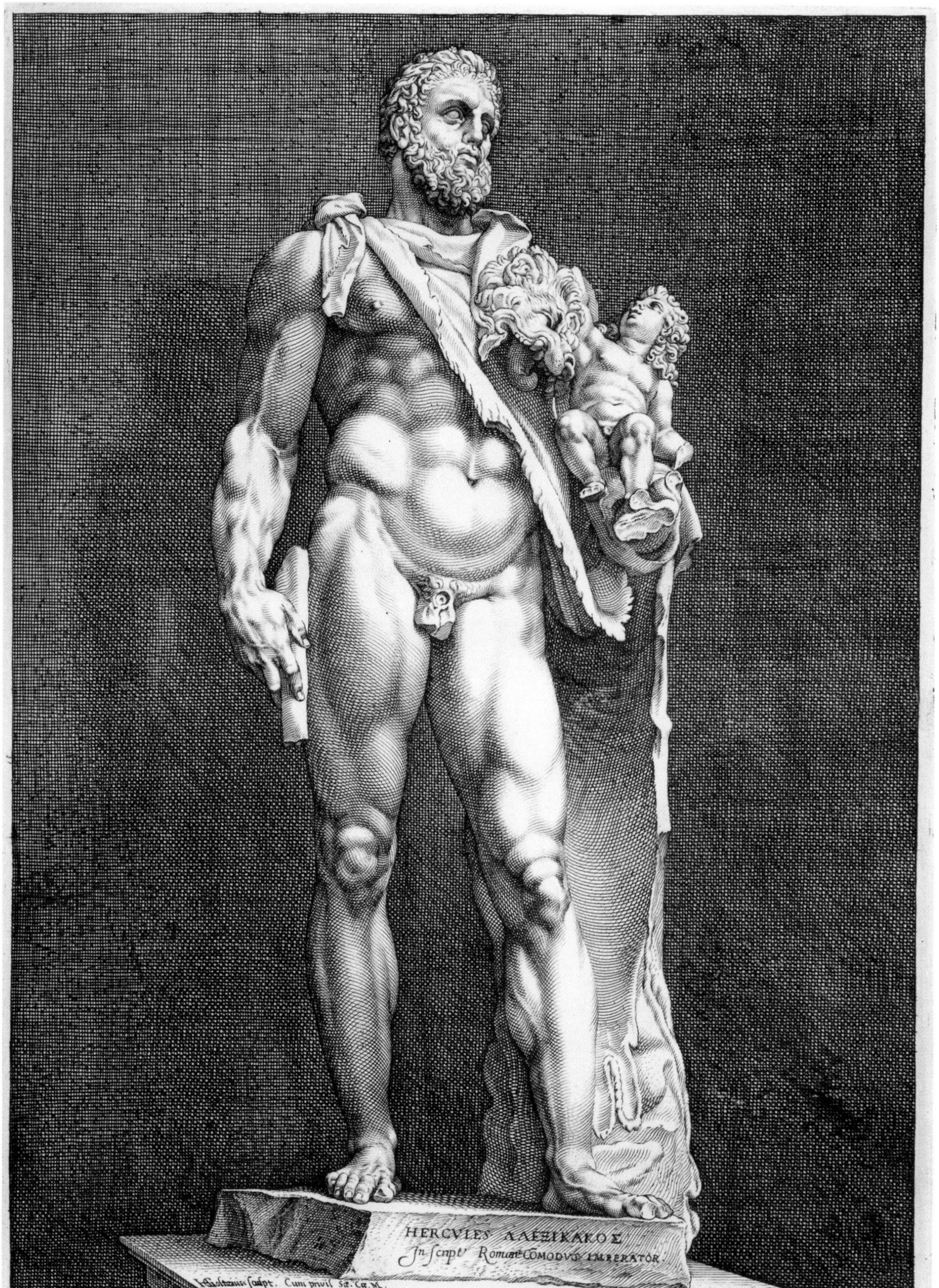
HERCVLES ΑΛΕΞΙΚΑΚΟΣ
In Scrpt. Roman. COMODVS IMPERATOR.
Cum privil. Sa. Ca. M.
Herman Adolfz. excud. Haerlemen.
Telamonis aulam victor Alcides subl.
Telamone natum Iovi, et Aiacem sinu
Statua antiqua Romæ in palatio Pontificis belle vider.
opus posthumum. Goltzy iam primum divulgatum An. M.D.C.XVII.
Spolys leonis implicans votum dedi,
Vt fata corpus vulnere intactum darent.

By the second half of the sixteenth century, Rome had become an essential destination for many European artists. As Giovanni Battista Armenini (1525–1609) wrote in 1587 in his treatise on painting, "Youths from almost every part of the world went to Rome . . . [to study] the most famous ancient sculptures that most closely approach the true perfection of art, and which are still intact today."[2] In addition to the monuments that had survived the ravages of time, such as triumphal arches, commemorative columns, and colossal statues, a number of spectacular Roman marble sculptures were excavated during the course of the century. Such vestiges of imperial grandeur, whose significance had already been established by a variety of ancient authorities, provided late Renaissance and early Baroque painters, sculptors, and architects with an enormous repository of figurative compositions and formal motifs. Moreover, contemporary authors celebrated the achievements of those artists who mastered the principles and models offered by classical art.

Although ancient monuments could be seen in the Renaissance in such northern cities as Bonn, Cologne, Maastricht, and Trier, many German and Netherlandish artists were encouraged to travel to Rome in order to study firsthand the most renowned extant sculptures and buildings. Prior to his seven-month-long sojourn in the Eternal City in early 1591, Hendrik Goltzius (1558–1617) had access through his association with the so-called academy in his hometown of Haarlem to sketchbooks that recorded antiquities. During his visit to Rome, Goltzius also made drawings of classical statues, probably with the aim of publishing them as a series of prints. Even though only three of these works were subsequently engraved, the first of their kind in Dutch art, these carefully prepared prints were greatly admired by artists, antiquarians, and collectors who were interested in reconstructing an image of the antique past through surviving texts and artifacts.[3]

One of the prints from Goltzius's series depicted a slightly larger-than-life-size marble statue of the Emperor Commodus (161–192 CE) as Hercules (Figure 12), a Roman copy modeled after a Greek bronze dating from the fourth century BCE. Unearthed in 1507 in the heart of the city's most populated neighborhood, it was immediately acquired by the pope and soon afterwards put on display in the Vatican's Belvedere courtyard, Rome's most prestigious sculpture collection. The engraving faithfully reproduced two of Goltzius's preparatory drawings, which exaggerated the proportions of the actual figure in order to record its appearance from the point of view of the observer. It seems that Goltzius was just as interested in demonstrating his understanding of the statue's original function and how it was intended to be seen as he was in recording its formal features. Such a perspective was typical of a number of artists of the same period, like Annibale Carracci (1560–1609) and Peter Paul Rubens (1577–1640), who utilized their thorough command of ancient art for the purpose of recreating the experience of viewing individual objects within a broader classical milieu.

From around 1600 onwards, the study of Roman antiquities became a central tenet of the art academies that were founded throughout Europe. For foreign institutions that did not have easy access to original works of art, prints and drawings of ancient monuments and sculptures, as well as casts made of life-sized and over-life-sized statues, were an important resource. In one case, the effort to

12
Hendrik Goltzius (1558–1617), *The Emperor Commodus as Hercules*, engraving, about 1591–92, printed 1617, purchased through the Jean and Adolph Weil Jr. 1935 Fund; PR.999.37

secure these types of reproductions led to the establishment in 1666 of a branch of the French Academy in Rome. In exchange for a full three- or four-year scholarship to record the marvels of antiquity, students were required to produce and send to Paris copies and casts of all the most valuable objects in Rome. The scheme not only helped to defer the costs of acquiring expensive reproductions, but it also provided an endless supply of works for various royal residences and institutions.

One beneficiary of this system was François-André Vincent (1746–1816), who left for Rome in 1771 and returned to Paris in 1775. His drawing of the famous bust of Lucius Junius Brutus (lived about 500 BCE) in the Capitoline Museum was undoubtedly made during his residency at the Academy, probably around 1774 (Figure 13). It depicts one of the city's most celebrated antiquities, the bronze portrait of the man who established republican government in Rome in the sixth century BCE. Vincent transformed a routine sketch into an impressive tour de force. Of the many busts, paintings, and book illustrations directly based on this sculpture, the French artist's rendering of the legendary Roman hero seemed to highlight the figure's distinctive character, which was described by one contemporary viewer as "melancholy, deep thought, firmness of soul, severity."[4] His work reflected the recurring interest in utilizing classical objects and motifs not only as figurative models but also as a means of expressing specific ideals.

The importance attached to young artists' appreciation of the supremacy of ancient art is perhaps best represented in a drawing executed around 1682 by Carlo Maratta (1625–1713), the most highly regarded painter in late-seventeenth-century Rome. Nicolas Dorigny (1657–1746) engraved the so-called *Academy of Painting* in reverse around 1702–03, and in 1728 it was published along with a lengthy, unsigned text (Figure 14). Maratta depicts an academic setting with pupils learning perspective, geometry, optics, and anatomy—then considered basic branches of art instruction. Under each of these disciplines are inscribed the words *Tanto che basti* ("No more than necessary"). The explicit message to students is that they need to understand and apply the principles of each area of knowledge, but they should not exercise any one of them too much. By comparison, adjacent to a group of apparently identifiable antique statues displayed in the background, Maratta emphasizes the aspiring painters' debt to antiquity with the words *Non mai abbastanza* ("Never enough"). Inspired by three graces with the motto *Senza di noi ogni fattica è vana* ("Without us every effort is pointless"), alluding to the divine gift of gracious composition, one is left to contemplate the statues as preeminent examples of artistic perfection without the aid of an instructor.

While both Hercules and Venus in this image were recognizable antique types based on known marbles, the central statue of Apollo holding a lyre was modeled after a fictive sculpture appearing in a niche on the left side of the *School of Athens* painted in 1510–11 by Raphael (1483–1520; Figure 8). When Maratta executed this work, Raphael had been considered the supreme embodiment of the classically trained artist for more than 150 years—and would be for centuries to follow. Along with the ancients, he symbolized the effort to imitate nature and to raise the art of assimilation to noble perfection. Maratta, who was coincidentally in charge of the conservation of the rooms in the Vatican containing Raphael's masterpiece, rendered the figure of Apollo as a free-standing, three-dimensional creation, thereby elevating its status to the level of the greatest works of antiquity and presenting it as an ideal model for young painters to emulate.

13
François-André Vincent (1746–1816), *Bust of Lucius Junius Brutus (The Capitoline Brutus)*, red chalk and wash, 1774, purchased through a gift from the Cremer Foundation in memory of J. Theodor Cremer and a gift from John W. Thompson, Class of 1908 and Dorothy M. Litzinger, by exchange; D.988.16

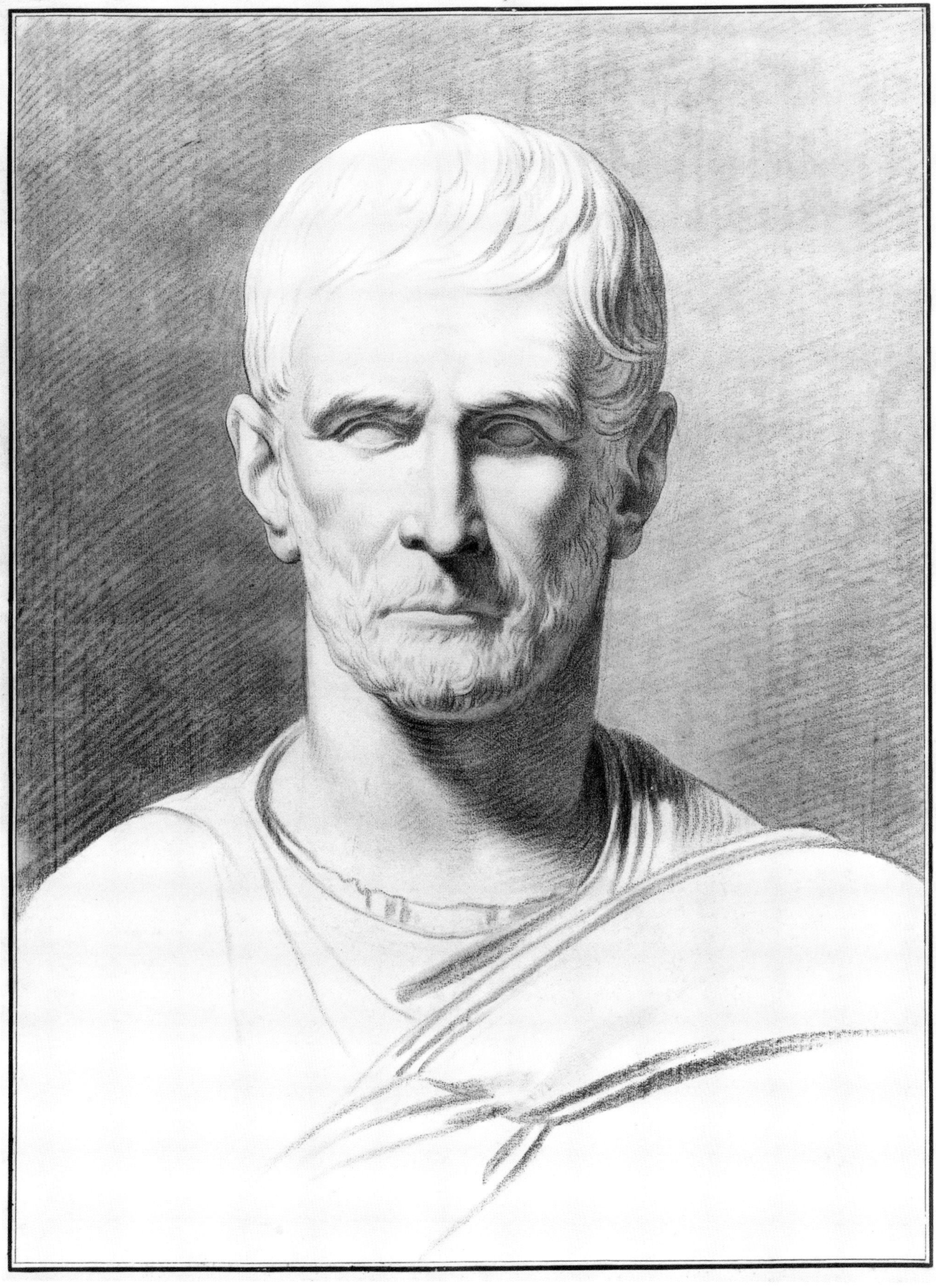

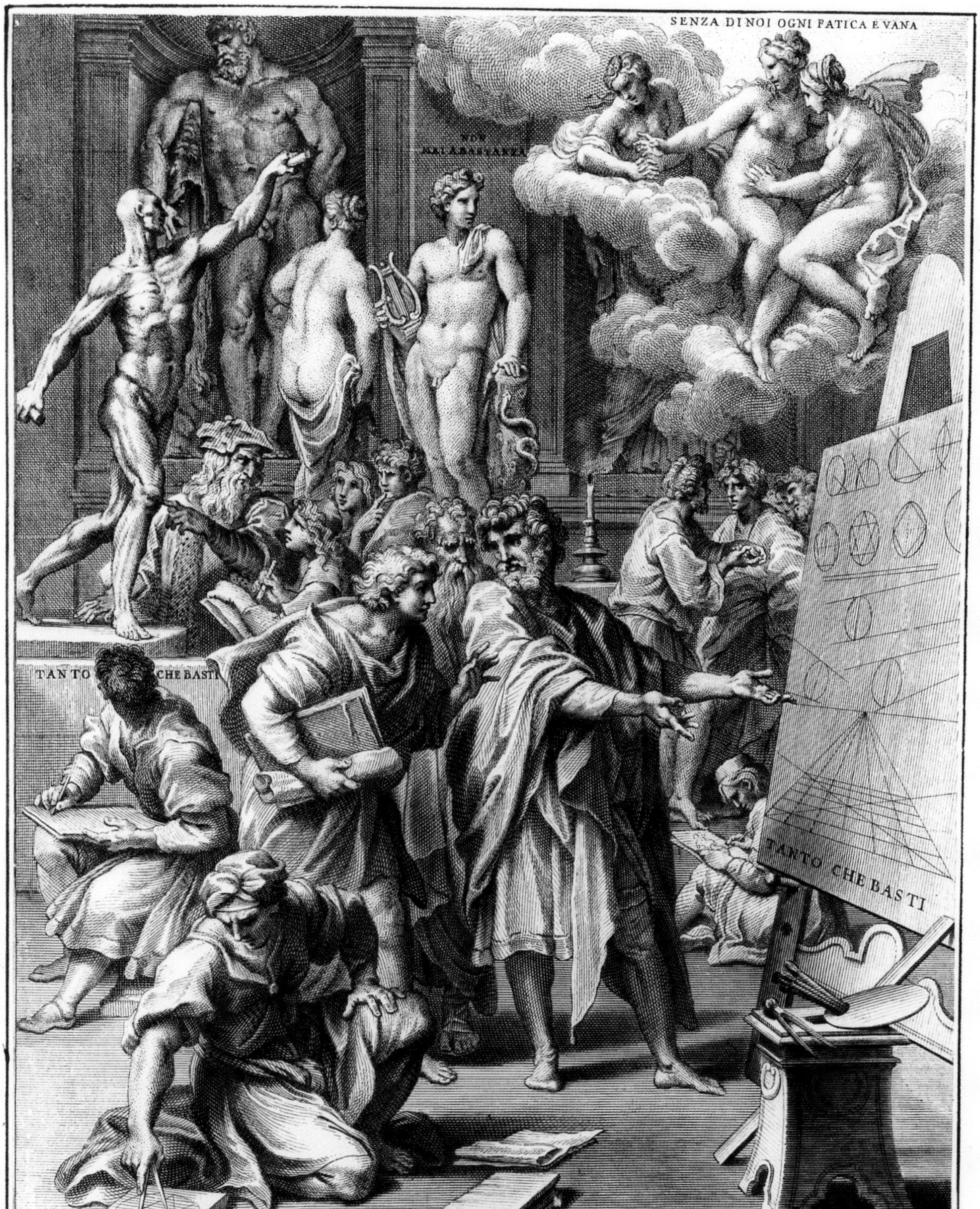

A Giouani studiosi del Disegno

La Scuola del Disegno, che s'espone delineata con le presenti Figure dal Sig.r Caualier Carlo Maratti, può molto contribuire al disinganno di coloro, che credono di potere con la cognizione, e ſtudio di molte Arti diuenir perfet.ti nell'Arte del dipingere senza procurare in primo luogo d'eſser perfettiſsimi nel Disegno, e ſenza il dono naturale, et un particolare istinto di ſaper con grazia, e facilità animare, e disporre uagamente le parti di quell'Opera, che prenderanno a delineare, e uà figurando questo ſuo nobil pensiero con il mezzo dell'azzioni, che qui ſi additano. Vedonsi alcuni ſtudiosi delle mathematiche in quella parte, che ſpetta alla Geometria, et Ottica, che conferiscono alla Prospettiua: dall'altro lato, altri applicati all'oſseruazione d'un Corpo anatomico, dà cui ſi apprende la giusta proporzione delle membra, e ſito de' muscoli, e nerui, che compongono una figura, dimostrato eruditamẽte dà Leonardo da Vinci eſpreſſo cõ la propria effigie, con il motto. Tanto che basti. per dimostrare, che di tali profeſsio.ni basta, che quello, che attenderà al Disegno ſia mediocrem.te erudito, per ridurre ad un perfetto fine qualunque Idea. Mà per coloro, che si esprimono attenti allo studio delle Statue antiche, non ſerue una leggiera applicazione ai le med.e, eſsendo lor d'uopo di farui ſopra una lunga, et esatta riſleſsione, e studio per apprenderne le belle forme; e ſi pone l'esemplare delle ſtatue antiche, come le più perfette, nelle quali quei grandi Huomini espressero i Corpi nel più perfetto grado, che poſsano dalla natura iſteſsa crearsi, e perciò ui si pone il motto. Non mai a bastanza. Tutto però riuscirebbe vano di conseguire ſenza l'aſsistenza delle Grazie, che intende, come accennammo, per quel natural gusto di disporre, et atteggiare con grazia, e delicatezza le positure, et i mouimenti delle Figure, dalle quali poi risulta quella uaghezza, e leggiadria, che destano merauiglia, e piacere in chiunque le mira, ponendosi queste a tal oggetto in alto, e ſù le nuuole per ſignificare, che questo dono non uiene che dal Cielo, con il motto. Senza di noi ogni fatica e vana. Viue felici.

Eques Carolus Maratti inuen. et delin. Cum priuil. Summi Pont. et Regis Christ.mi

N. Dorigny ſculp.

Along with the revival of classical principles of art, a growing number of historians, archeologists, and theologians sought to chronicle and catalog ancient history, artifacts, and rites. They considered the physical remains of Rome's past an important complement to its surviving literary legacy and carefully documented and studied its inscriptions, coins, ruins, and other relics. Gradually, systematic excavations replaced random discoveries, while existing collections were often reorganized according to different didactic criteria. Concurrently, the circulation of vast quantities of drawings, prints, and illustrated publications reproducing both notable monuments and common objects sustained an expanding international community of connoisseurs. The development of these antiquarian pursuits eventually led to the birth of modern archeology and art history.

At the same time, the prominence of classical scholarship attracted the attention of royalty and nobility all over Europe. Motivated by both aesthetic and ideological interests, they formed collections and founded academies and societies. A wave of affluent foreign tourists and dignitaries swept Rome to observe personally the grandeur of the ancient city, which also stimulated a burgeoning market for antiquities and reproductions. These objects were acquired throughout the continent by a large number of upper-class families, some of whom genuinely cultivated the revival of ancient art and traditions, while others simply cultivated their social status.

Nearly every socially and politically important visitor to the Eternal City was accompanied by a learned guide, also known as a *cicerone*, who would have shown them the most significant sites and discoveries. In addition, early handbooks, which were frequently illustrated, described the historical settings and often recreated the original splendor of selected artifacts. Giovanni Alto, or Hans Alt (died around 1652), whose portrait was engraved in 1623 by Francesco Villamena (about 1565–1624; Figure 15), was a Swiss resident in Rome involved both in leading foreigners around on tours and in the publishing of such books. Identified in the inscription at the bottom of the sheet as a "researcher and guide to the antiquities," Alto chose to portray himself situated in a prominent position overlooking the city and gesturing towards some of its most famous monuments, such as the pair of second-century colossal marble *Dioscuri*, or "Horsetamers," on the Quirinal Hill. Several years after this print appeared, Alto published an expanded edition of Giacomo Lauro's *Ancient Splendors of Rome*, a medium-sized volume that included illustrations of hypothetical reconstructions of significant monuments and views of major ruins. The potential market for Alto's publication and portrait would have been tourists who wanted a record of the sites they had seen and a personal memento of their guide.

The engraved portrait was dedicated to Cassiano dal Pozzo (1588–1657), a friend of the printmaker who was renowned internationally as the foremost antiquarian in seventeenth-century Rome. During the course of many years, dal Pozzo engaged many well- and lesser-known artists to prepare thousands of drawings of all sorts of ancient objects, from works of art to simple utensils, which were cataloged according to their subject matter and formed a visual encyclopedia of surviving Roman antiquities. Bound in volumes, the collection was later described by dal Pozzo as his "Paper Museum." Throughout this enterprise, he exchanged

14
Nicolas Dorigny (1652/58–1746), after Carlo Maratta (1625–1713), *The Academy of Painting*, engraving, 1728, collection of Robert Dance, Class of 1977

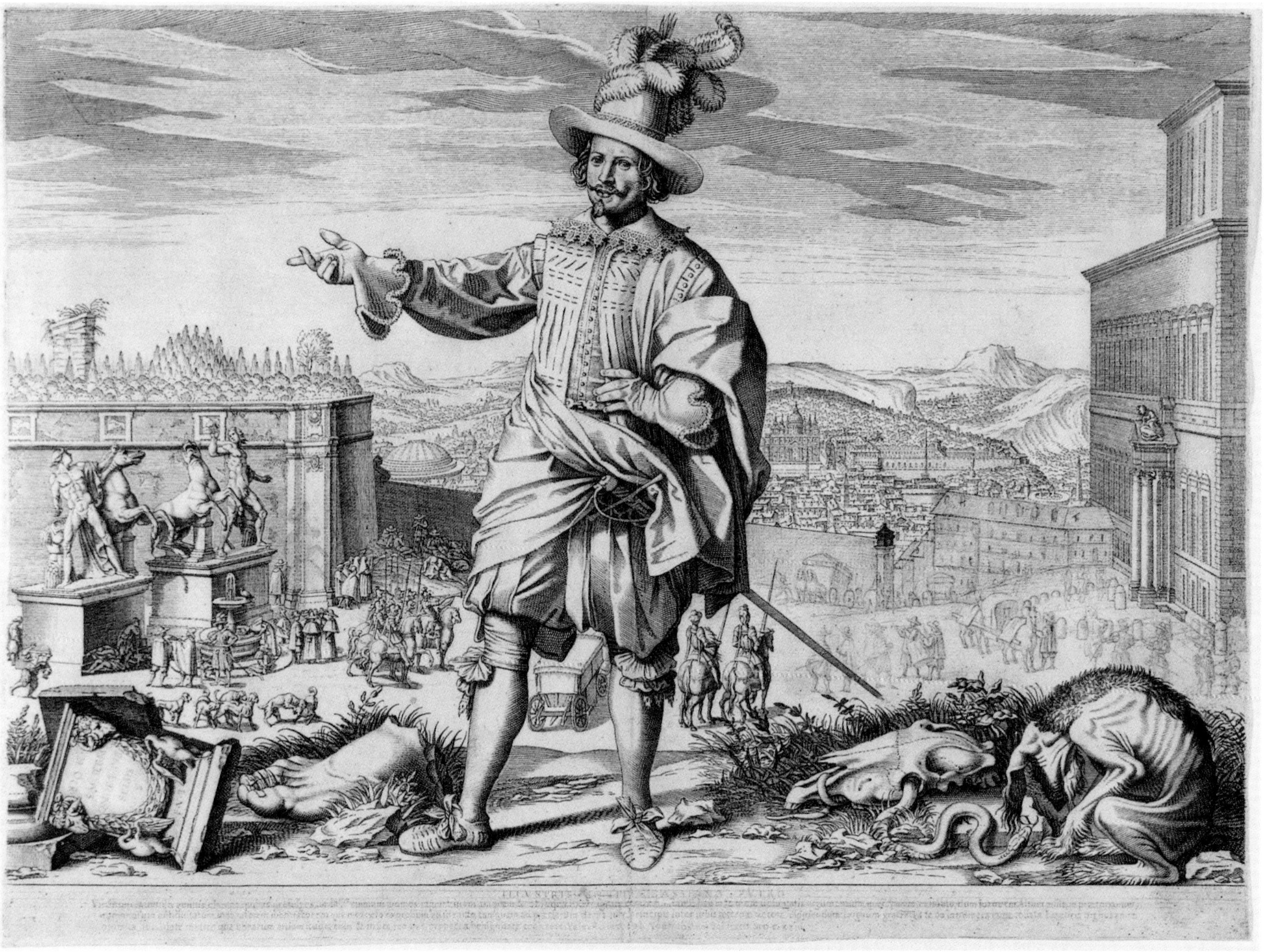

15
Francesco Villamena (1566–1624), *Portrait of Giovanni Alto, Antiquarian*, engraving with red and black chalk, 1623, purchased through the Class of 1935 Memorial Fund and the Jean and Adolph Weil Jr. 1935 Fund; PR.997.29.2

letters and other materials with scholars around Europe in an effort to document and interpret his discoveries. His correspondence indicated the extent to which he and his colleagues understood the importance of printmaking for their investigations as well as for the dissemination of their findings. Despite his intentions, the Paper Museum was never published, but a number of sheets were reproduced by other authors, and his collection served as an essential resource for many artists and scholars until its dispersal in the eighteenth century.

Dal Pozzo's commitment to the investigation of the remains of Roman civilization was motivated primarily by his desire to uncover the greatest intrinsic values of the classical world. His dedication and vision inspired others to carry out similar pursuits, such as the long list of antiquarian and archeological publications organized by Giovanni Pietro Bellori (1613–1696) and featuring prints by Pietro Santi Bartoli (about 1635–1700). These works marked a high point in the history of illustrated books of antiquities, which were distinguished by the precision of the images and the erudition of the Latin descriptions. One of the most popular publications that they produced was *Extraordinary Antiquities of Rome*, first printed around 1677 and reissued in an expanded form in 1693 (Figure 16). As stated in the title, this series of annotated engravings reproduced a selective group of marbles drawn from the most celebrated collections in Rome. The owners of these ancient works of art especially valued the implicit aesthetic and historical judgement associated with this selection. As one late-seventeenth-century observer noted, wealthy collectors supported the dissemination of reproductions of their most prized antiquities in order to publicize their own *vitù*, or virtues.[5]

While artists were encouraged to draw aesthetic inspiration from classical works of art, noble men and women were generally expected to become virtuosi through an appreciation and understanding of the relics of the past as "illustrations of antient [*sic*] history and literature."[6] Consequently, many affluent families around Europe formed somewhat large-sized collections of original antiquities. One of the earliest and most important in England was established by Thomas Herbert, eighth earl of Pembroke (1656–1733). At the family estate at Wilton House, Herbert assembled a collection of nearly 250 statues, busts, and reliefs between 1678 and 1726. Some of the finest sculptures were purchased in Rome during a trip in the late seventeenth century, while other marbles were obtained from a few of the most well-known holdings throughout the continent. In 1731, Herbert selected seventy objects to be engraved and issued in a single volume.

By the time the publication appeared, Herbert's entire collection was displayed in different rooms according to an arrangement that remained largely unchanged for nearly 180 years (before the building was dramatically renovated in the early nineteenth century). Eventually, Dartmouth College acquired one of the sarcophagus reliefs from Wilton House in 1977 (Figure 17). Unfortunately, the earliest eighteenth-century inventories did not record the original provenance of the marble or the date that it entered Herbert's collection. Nonetheless, they did indicate that the iconography of the sculpture was clearly recognized as a depiction of Nereids and Tritons (confirmed by a later inscription, possibly added in the sixteenth or seventeenth century, at the bottom: ΝΗΡΕΙΔΕΣ). These figures were known from classical mythology as sea nymphs and hybrid creatures typically engaged in sensuous games in aquatic settings. In Renaissance and Baroque visual and literary interpretations, the funerary function of the sarcophagus was often ignored in favor

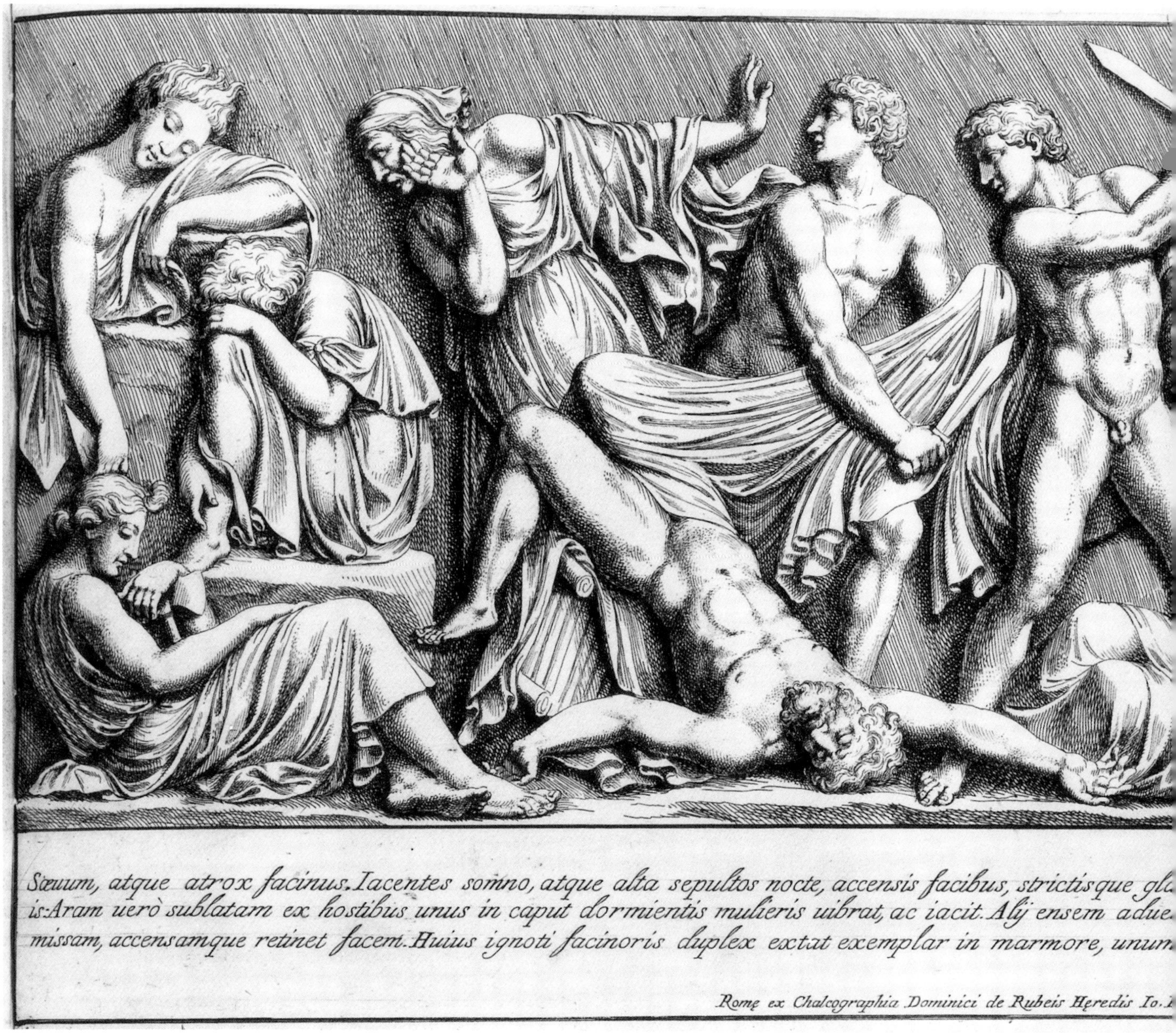

16
Pietro Santi Bartoli (1635–1700), after unknown, Roman (active second century CE), *Roman Sarcophagus Representing Orestes' Revenge*, engraving, in Bartoli, *Admiranda romanarum antiquitatum* . . . (Rome, 1693), pl. 52, collection of Dartmouth College Library

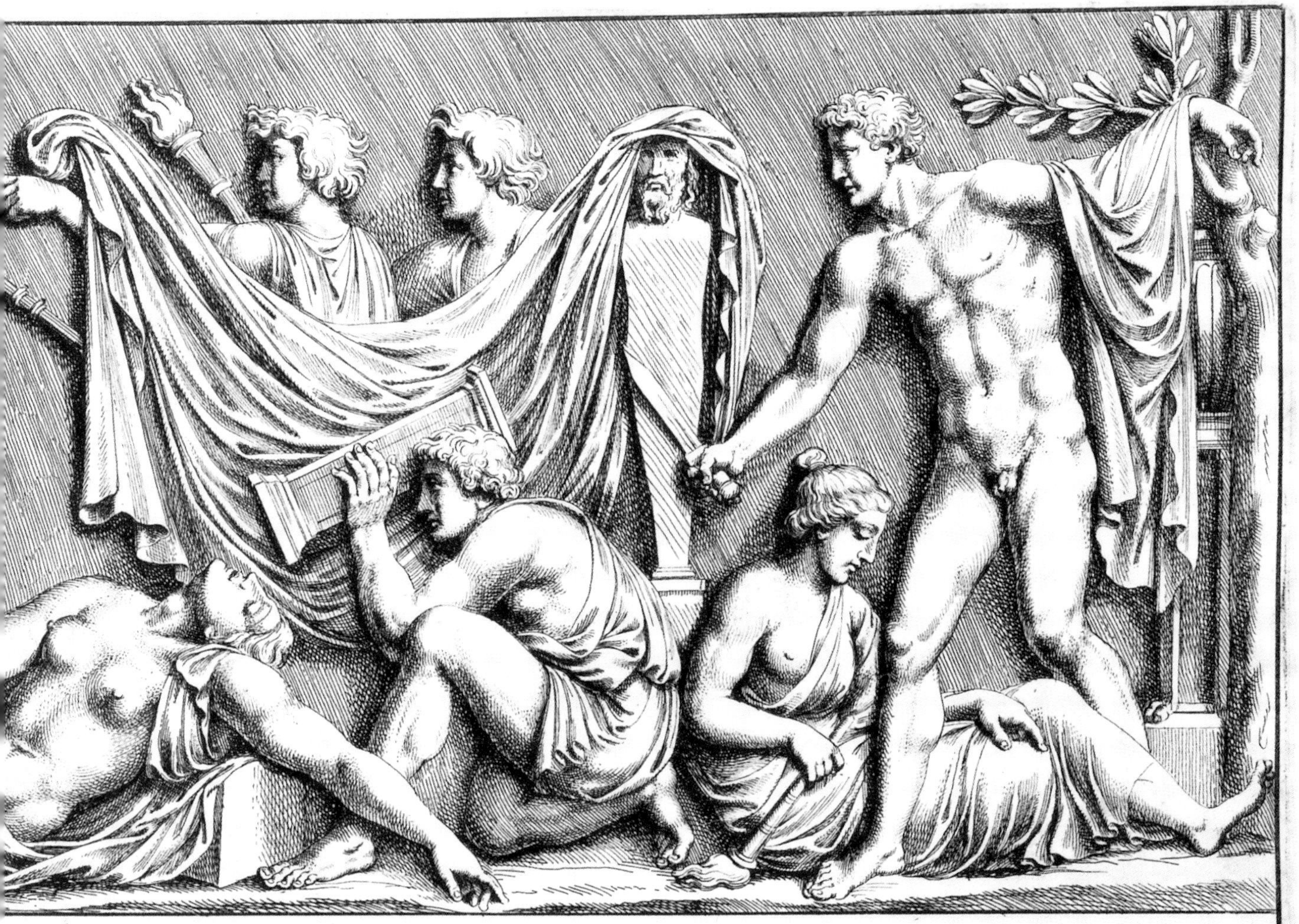

repentino impetu inuadunt. Termini Dei solemnia peragunt, posito eius simulacro, ac tripode cum aulę=
ntes ad necem intendunt. Hinc Sacrificę duę iacentes sopore grauatę, altera securi nititur, altera di=
inis, alterum in Iustinianis ędibus, à quo similitudinem duximus.

ad Templ. S. Marię de Pace cum Priu. S.P. et Super. perm. *In Aedibus Iustinianis* 52

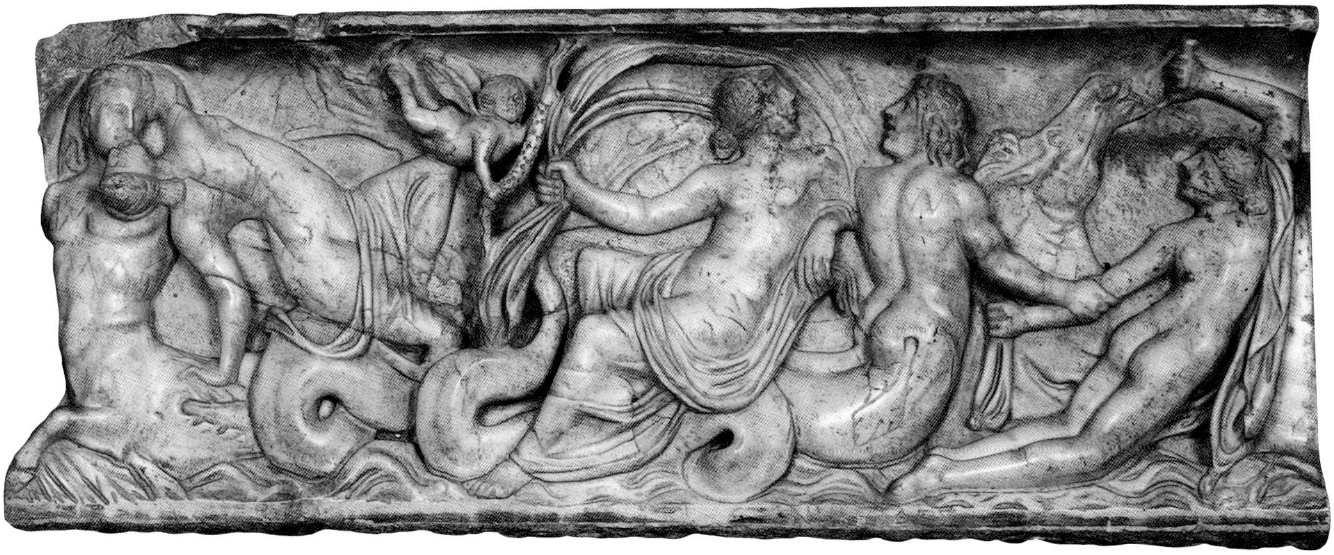

17
Unknown, Roman (second century CE), *Sarcophagus Fragment: Eros with Nereids and Tritons*, marble, about 140–160 CE, Acquisitions Fund; s.977.21

of the erotic attraction of the nudes in artful poses. Based on inventories of the other sculptures representing similar themes adjacent to this relief in the Stone Hall at Wilton House, which was used as the ceremonial entrance on the ground floor of the south wing, Herbert's installation appeared to have been consciously organized to create certain associations. In contrast to Cassiano dal Pozzo's visual encyclopedia, the Earl of Pembroke utilized his collection of antiquities as a selected repertory of classical subjects for edifying entertainment.

THE "IDEA" OF CLASSICAL BEAUTY IN THE SEVENTEENTH CENTURY

By the seventeenth century, virtually all artists were aware of the art of antiquity to an even greater extent than their predecessors were. Earlier generations were neither less enthusiastic nor less diligent, but the increasingly systematic study of classical art became more common and accessible. Even those who had firsthand knowledge from their brief visits or extended sojourns in Rome were able to draw on numerous additional resources. As has already been noted, such studies were aided by the increased circulation of prints and books illustrating and explicating ancient history and culture. These phenomena contributed to the formulation of new critical interpretations and the emergence of various ideal types and forms. For many seventeenth-century artists, classical antiquity represented the perfect combination of art and nature, but the slavish imitation of specific exempla was rebuked in favor of a greater role for judicious imagination based on the most accomplished models.

Nicolas Poussin (1594–1665), the principal painter of this period who best reflected the new attitude toward the ancient world, left Paris in 1624 for Rome, where he spent practically the rest of his lifetime. Poussin did not aspire to idealize classical forms or to recreate the physical splendors of antiquity. Instead, he attempted to give visual expression to the artistry and mystery of antique subjects through his profound understanding of their cultural manifestations. He applied the same degree of empathy and antiquarian spirit to his representations of biblical themes, reflecting an interest that was more archeological than doctrinal. He approached both profane and sacred paintings as history, which he attempted to reconstruct by using the most up-to-date information. This knowledge was largely based on his close contact and collaboration with collectors and scholars such as Cassiano dal Pozzo and Giovanni Pietro Bellori—who were, not surprisingly, also his patrons.

Among Poussin's most celebrated works is one that depicts a biblical scene based on the story of Eliezer and Rebecca (Genesis 24: 22–27), which was painted for a Parisian client in 1648 and subsequently engraved—in the same orientation—less than thirty years later, after the painting entered the royal collection (Figure 18). The diversity of the expressions, the variety of the gestures and poses, and the satisfactory relationship between the foreground and background have been repeatedly noted by both contemporary and modern observers (including Jean-Auguste-Dominique Ingres [1780–1867] and Pablo Picasso [1881–1973], who reproduced its simplicity and formal purity in partial painted copies). In addition, others have identified a number of individual antique references based on promi-

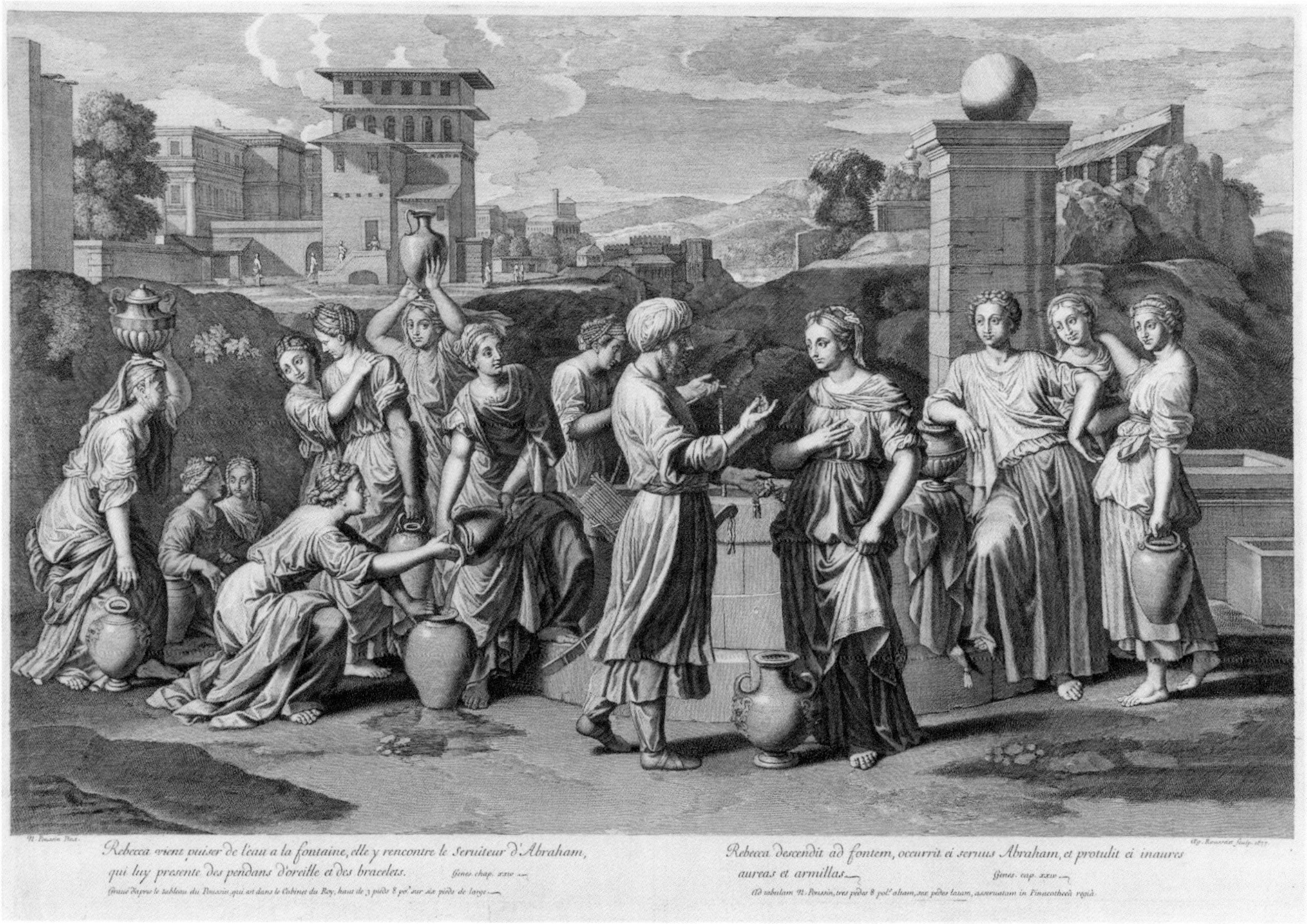

18
Gilles Rousselet (1610–1686), after Nicolas Poussin (1594–1665), *Eliezer and Rebecca at the Well*, engraving, 1677, purchased through the Guernsey Center Moore 1904 Memorial Fund, the Class of 1935 Memorial Fund, the Mrs. Harvey P. Hood W'18 Fund, and the Julia L. Whittier Fund; PR.997.3.4

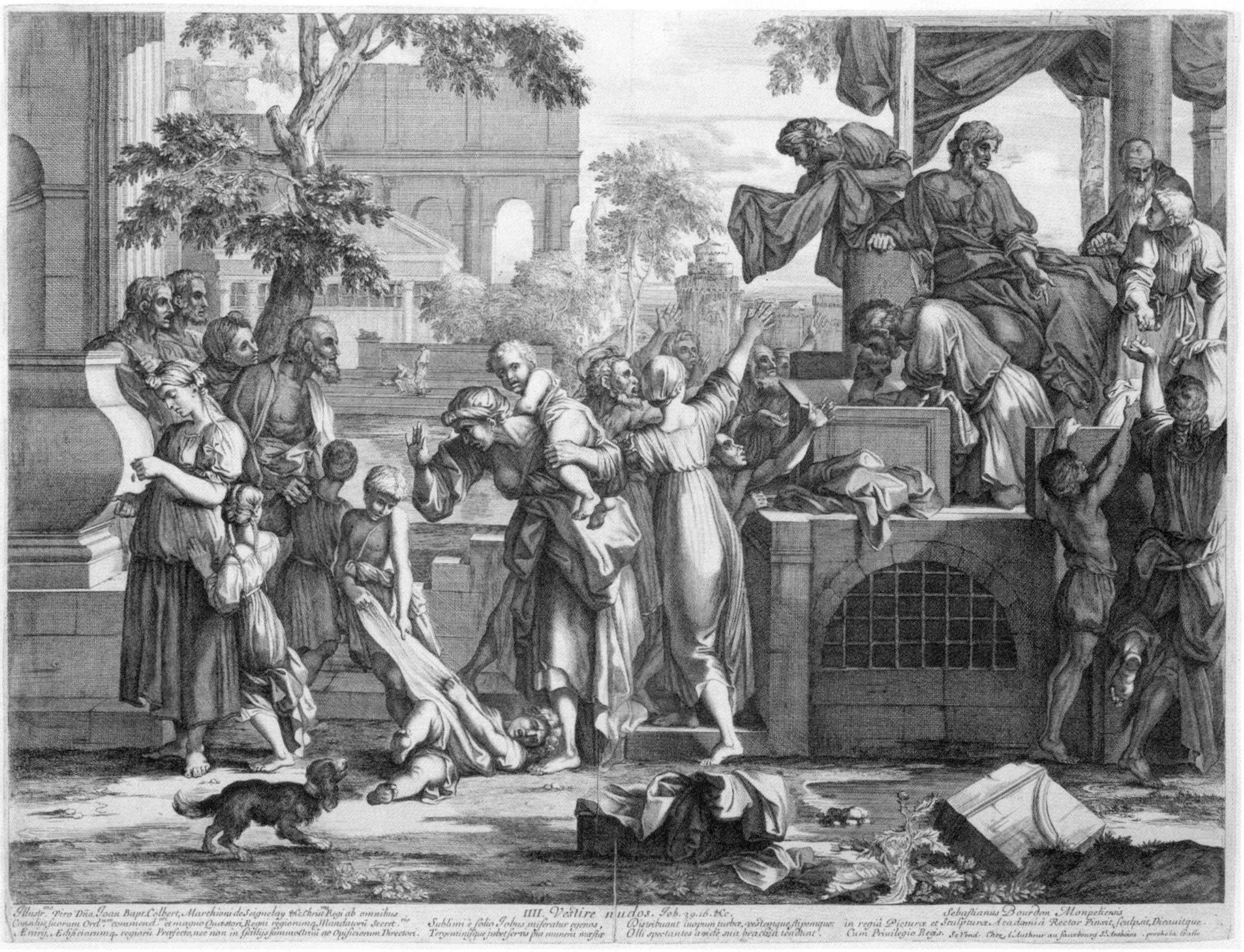

19

Sebastien Bourdon (1616–1671), *Clothe the Naked (Vestire nudos)*, from the series *Acts of Mercy*, etching and engraving, about 1665–70, purchased through the Julia L. Whittier Fund; PR.971.6.4

nent works of art in Rome that Poussin clearly had seen and studied. In fact, nearly all of his painted figures from the 1640s have the character of ancient statues. Yet, even though he is known to have made antiquity "his chief study," as Gian Lorenzo Bernini (1598–1680) once said of him, Poussin almost always alters slightly the position and proportions of his borrowed figures in order to create new compositions.[7] He uses these apparently explicit references to represent different ideal characteristics or types, such as harmonious proportions or old age, rather than selecting them for their ability to recall specific models.

Poussin's artistic notions epitomized the concepts elaborated by Bellori, who considered the French painter to be the paradigmatic artist of his day. Bellori first presented his thoughts in a lecture delivered at the Academy of St. Luke in Rome in 1664 and later expanded them in his biographies of famous painters, sculptors, and architects, initially published in 1672. Like Poussin, Bellori saw the art of the ancients as a guide to follow in the selection of the most superb elements from nature in order to create the "idea" of perfect beauty in the imagination of the artist and the spectator. In both men's minds, their admiration for antiquity was limitless, but that did not imply that they would follow its example blindly. They aspired to discover the true laws of art, and they considered classical models to be the most perfect embodiments of ideal nature.

Poussin's reputation for depicting ideal forms, human actions, and expressive emotions within highly accurate historical settings influenced generations of artists and critics in both Italy and France. Even in his day, painters throughout Europe marveled at his achievements, which were to be seen in many notable collections, while teachers at the French Academy in Paris emulated his principles. One artist who taught at the academy and had adopted Poussin's intellectual program and formal vocabulary was Sébastien Bourdon (1616–1671), who worked primarily in Paris after a three-year stay in Rome in the mid-1630s. In one particular example, Bourdon painted a series of seven scenes in the late 1660s entitled *Acts of Mercy* (Figure 19) that was directly inspired by Poussin's second series entitled *The Sacraments*, originally executed in Rome in the mid-1640s for a client in Paris. In terms of style, subject matter, and general dimensions, the two sets were very similar. Moreover, they shared the same general classicizing imagery, with foreground figures arranged in various architectural surroundings.

In Bourdon's fourth act, *To Clothe the Naked* (based on episodes in Job 31: 19–20 and Matthew 25: 35–36), illustrated here, the urban background contains recognizable Roman types and fragments, such as the upper portion of the Colosseum on the left. The formula for using cities and landscapes as the stage for human activity is derived from ancient reliefs, in which harmonious settings are often used as a backdrop to dramatic mythological and historical tales. Similarly, Bourdon's scene follows a long tradition of recreating the imperial city as an acceptable site for recording such noble acts. In addition, the poses, expressions, and groupings of the figures convey a distinct aura of Roman paganism to a biblical story.

The evocative power of ancient surroundings and artifacts played a significant role in the paintings of another French artist living in seventeenth-century Rome, Claude Lorrain (1604/05–1682), considered the greatest ideal landscape painter. Beginning in the first half of the century in the Eternal City, there was a marked increase in the production of works of art depicting landscapes, most of them executed by northern Europeans. On the one hand, foreign artists were inspired

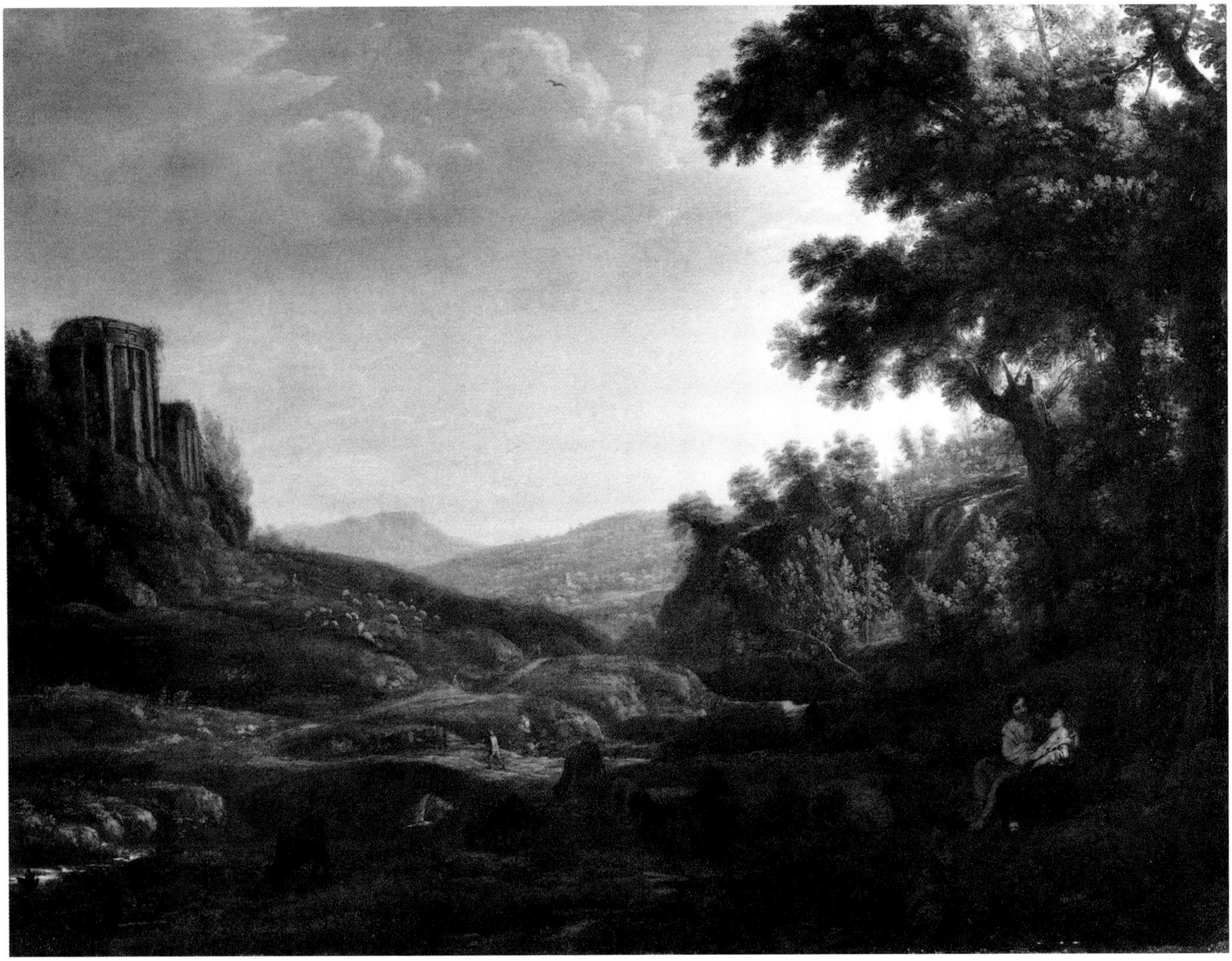

20

Claude Lorrain (1600–1682), *Landscape with a Shepherd and Shepherdess*, oil on canvas, about 1636, purchased through gifts from Peter and Kirsten Bedford and Julia and Richard H. Rush, Class of 1937, and through the Mrs. Harvey P. Hood W'18 Fund, the Guernsey Center Moore 1904 Memorial Fund, and the Merrill and Katherine Beede 1929 Fund, and through gifts by exchange; P.989.21

to study nature after seeing the heightened beauty of the idealized scenic views produced by Annibale Carracci and other Italians. On the other hand, these typically smaller pictures of the Roman countryside and its ancient ruins were popular with upper-class residents and visitors. Both factors contributed to the establishment of landscape painting as an independent genre.

In his early work, Claude often combined fantastic natural settings and familiar architectural elements to evoke pastoral and classical themes (Figure 20). The resulting imaginary effect was frequently accentuated by the appearance of shepherds and shepherdesses in modern clothing, who seemed to symbolize the human condition in an uncultivated environment. Compared to an artist like Poussin, for whom figures in open landscapes suggested a heroic harmony of nature and civilized virtues, Claude aimed to create more romantic and picturesque impressions. An integral feature of these images was the appearance of apparently recognizable monuments in ruins situated in ideal contexts, especially the Temple of the Sibyl at Tivoli (which the artist is known to have visited on at least one occasion in the mid-1630s in the company of Poussin and other northern European artists).[8] As a result, these ancient structures recalled the heritage of the past, while minimizing their specific archeological significance.

According to the artist's records, an unknown client in Paris commissioned the Hood Museum of Art's painting by Claude. Not surprisingly, the Earl of Pembroke also acquired works of art by both Poussin and Claude for Wilton House, which were appropriately situated in the midst of his incredible collection of Roman antiquities. Following a well-established tradition of the sixteenth and seventeenth centuries, collectors expressed their taste for classical culture in both amateur antiquarianism and contemporary patronage.

CLASSICAL TRADITIONS IN THE EIGHTEENTH CENTURY

The eighteenth century in Rome witnessed a continued general enthusiasm for collecting and connoisseurship, but gradually a group of scholars emerged who made the study of antiquity their principal interest. As one of the founders of the nascent field of "archeological science" described it, "archaeology is the fruit of a judicious reading of the classics, of a diligent comparison of monuments, of a sure taste for the fine arts, a deep knowledge of the customs, laws, religion, and the character of the ancient peoples, a knowledge which is not distinct from philosophy."[9] One consequence of this movement was that the study of antiquities began to distance itself from contemporary artistic trends, thereby privileging historical principles over aesthetic ideals. This phenomenon did not, however, diminish artists' fascination with classical art. On the contrary, painters, sculptors, and architects followed these developments with great interest, but they largely used new discoveries to refine a formal vocabulary that ultimately sought to define the essence of classicism.

The shift toward more critical interpretations of the surviving body of ancient relics began with *An Account of Some of the Statues . . . in Italy*, first published in 1722 by Jonathan Richardson Sr. (1665–1745) and his son Jonathan Richardson Jr. (1694–1771), in which the two authors emphasized the significance of the antique sculptures that had been lost. They equated the total number of extant marbles to a few volumes washed ashore after a great library had been lost at sea. Moreover, they observed that the marbles that had survived were damaged and imperfect editions of earlier works.[10] Based on a comparison between examples known in the Renaissance and Baroque eras and those singled out as the greatest sculptures by ancient authorities, the Richardsons concluded that statues by the most famous classical artists had not survived. In addition, they discussed the problems of authenticity posed by the existence of multiple versions of the same sculpture, suggesting that they were all copies—of varying quality—of lost originals.

At the same time that the Richardsons published their conclusions, new reference works appeared in print. The largest of these books was the ten-part corpus of reproductions of ancient art entitled *Antiquity Explained and Represented in Sculptures*, produced between 1719 and 1724 by Bernard de Montfaucon (1655–1741). Like Cassiano dal Pozzo before him, Montfaucon commissioned artists to make copies of antique statues, reliefs, and other objects from every known source, as well as materials sent to him from antiquarians from around Europe. By the early 1720s, he estimated that he had collected thirty or forty thousand images. This voluminous pictorial encyclopedia was organized according to Montfaucon's own historical categories, with little regard for the objects' relative scale, artistic merit, and authenticity. In spite of its limitations, however, it remained an indispensable anthology for over a century.

Nearly fifty years after the appearance of the books by the Richardsons and Montfaucon, the general enthusiasm for classical culture was gradually replaced by a more systematic approach to the study of the ancient world. The focus of scholars such as Johann Joachim Winckelmann (1717–1768) shifted toward the development of stylistic and chronological classifications of antiquities, replacing traditional antiquarian interests aimed principally at subject matter. Winckelmann was a German who moved to Rome in 1755 and became librarian for one of the city's most influential cardinals and later the prefect of papal antiquities, providing him with extraordinary access to innumerable textual resources and unique visual evidence. Drawing on the intuitive conclusions of the Richardsons, Winckelmann applied his erudition toward the creation of a methodical account of the formal evolution of art—primarily sculpture—in both ancient Greece and Rome, which he published in 1764 as the *History of Ancient Art*.[11] The notion of a logical sequence of artistic periods, as well as the larger idea that art was a product of a historical process, established new paradigms for both archeologists and art historians.

Winckelmann's concepts influenced generations of future scholars, yet they also aided a new creative search for aesthetic purity. The previously indiscriminate use of antique motifs and models was replaced by greater historical and formal accuracy. Among the artists who applied their fascination with the latest archeological findings to the development of novel artistic inventions was Claude Michel, called Clodion (1738–1814). He arrived in Rome in 1762 after winning a three-year scholarship at the French Academy, eventually remaining in Italy for a period of nine years. Clodion and others in his circle were especially interested in the challenge of depicting three-dimensional representations with multiple figures in low relief (Figure 21), based primarily on extensive studies of ancient sarcophagi. Included in many of the these compositions were scenes of women making sacrifices, derived from extant ancient images and the written descriptions by

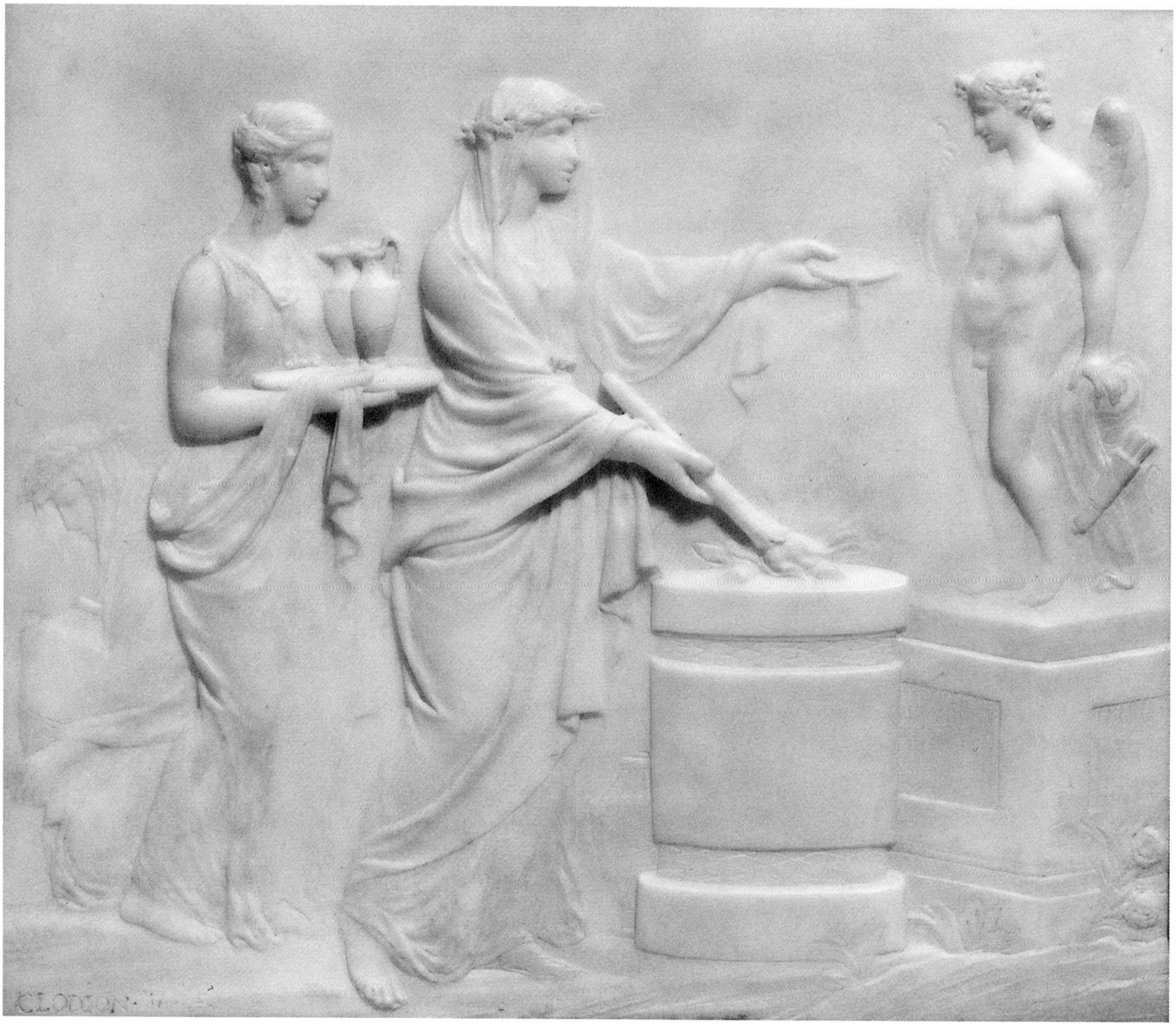

21
Claude Michel, called Clodion (1738–1814), *The Sacrifice to Cupid*, marble, about 1765–70, collection of Roger Arvid Anderson, Class of 1968; EL.S.998.28

Plutarch (about 46–120/25 CE) of the cult of Vesta, the Roman goddess of hearth and home. These allegorical narratives were immensely popular with both patrons and artists, who would have been familiar with such images through the publication of a number of examples uncovered recently at the ancient site of Herculaneum in Naples.[12]

Among the eighteenth-century artists working in Rome who derived their principal inspiration from profound knowledge and firsthand study of surviving antiquities was Giovanni Battista Piranesi (1720–1778). His vast production of prints reflected a unique combination of remarkable imagination and practical understanding of Roman architecture, which helped to disseminate and cultivate an unprecedented appreciation for the achievements of ancient Rome.

Throughout his career, Piranesi produced carefully prepared views and measured images of antique structures and ruins. Nevertheless, beginning in the 1760s, the contemporary debates over the superiority of Roman versus Greek art prompted the printmaker to highlight the greatest accomplishments of imperial Rome. According to Piranesi, one of the finest examples of the ancients' perfect blending of rich ornamentation and simple design was Trajan's Column, erected in 113 CE to commemorate some of the emperor's most important military campaigns (Figure 22).[13] The wealth of iconographic and stylistic information contained in the approximately 2,500 figures situated in various architectural and natural settings had served as an essential source for countless historians and artists since the fifteenth century. Several printmakers from the end of the sixteenth century onward had prepared complete sets of reproductions, which were consistently in high demand. Around 1774, Piranesi first published his series of detailed etchings of the entire column accompanied by explanatory texts. Yet, even though major sections were based on plaster casts that the artist had secured from the French Academy, he could not resist adding his own fanciful reconstruction of the missing free-standing statue of Trajan at the summit, which was recorded in an entirely different form—undoubtedly known by the artist—in numerous surviving coins (Figure 23). In spite of the presence of several accurately rendered relics from which the artist drew inspiration, the figurative and decorative composition was a fantastic creation that defied archeological explanation but captured the viewer's imagination.

Piranesi adopted the same strategy of presenting realistic archeological reconstructions imbued with an innovative creative spirit in several other works. Chief among them was his highly unusual series of prints called *Imaginary Prisons* (Figure 24). These etchings were first issued as a set of fourteen plates around 1749 and again, after significant reworking, as a set of sixteen in 1761. Basing his work on his extensive recordings of actual ancient subterranean structures in and around Rome, Piranesi composed imaginary views of antique-like underground spaces. Populated with indistinguishable figures that emphasized the scale and complexity of these spaces, the greater detail and stronger tonal contrasts of Piranesi's later edition exacerbated the images' sinister character. Even more importantly, while the first edition of capricious settings evoked the simplicity and utility for which Roman architecture was renowned, the second edition represented a conscious attempt to recreate the majesty and grandeur of antiquity. The immensity and ambiguity of these structures reinforced the sensation of wonderment, which Piranesi intentionally exaggerated in his realistic representations of existing

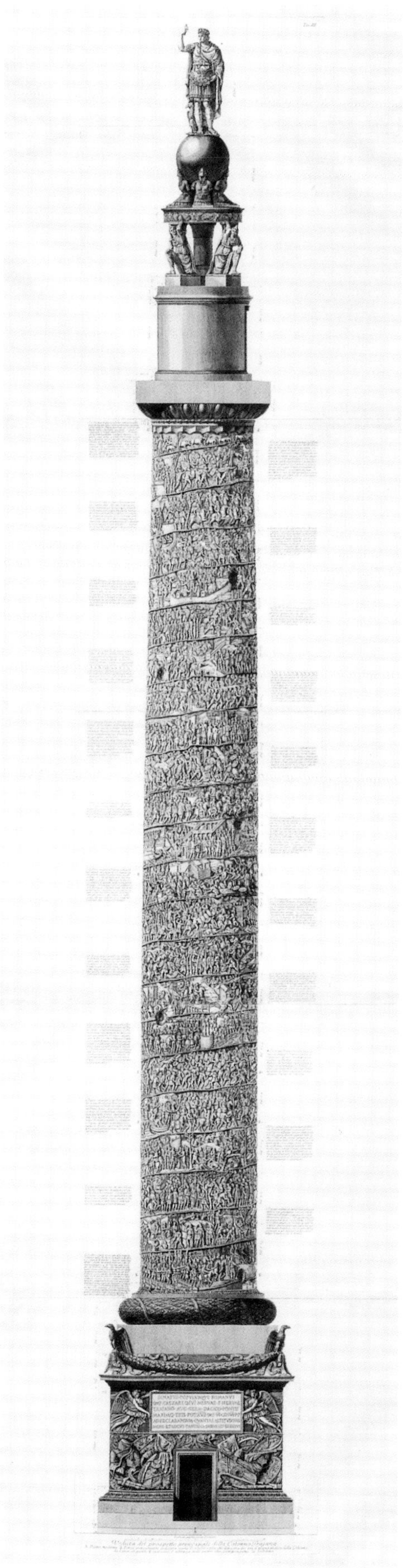

22
Giovanni Battista Piranesi (1720–1778), *View of the Principal Elevation of the Column of Trajan*, etching, about 1774, Hood Museum of Art, Dartmouth College; PR.967.130.3

23
Giovanni Battista Piranesi (1720–1778), *View of the Principal Elevation of the Column of Trajan* (detail showing the reconstruction of the Statue of Trajan), etching, about 1774, Hood Museum of Art, Dartmouth College; PR.967.130.3

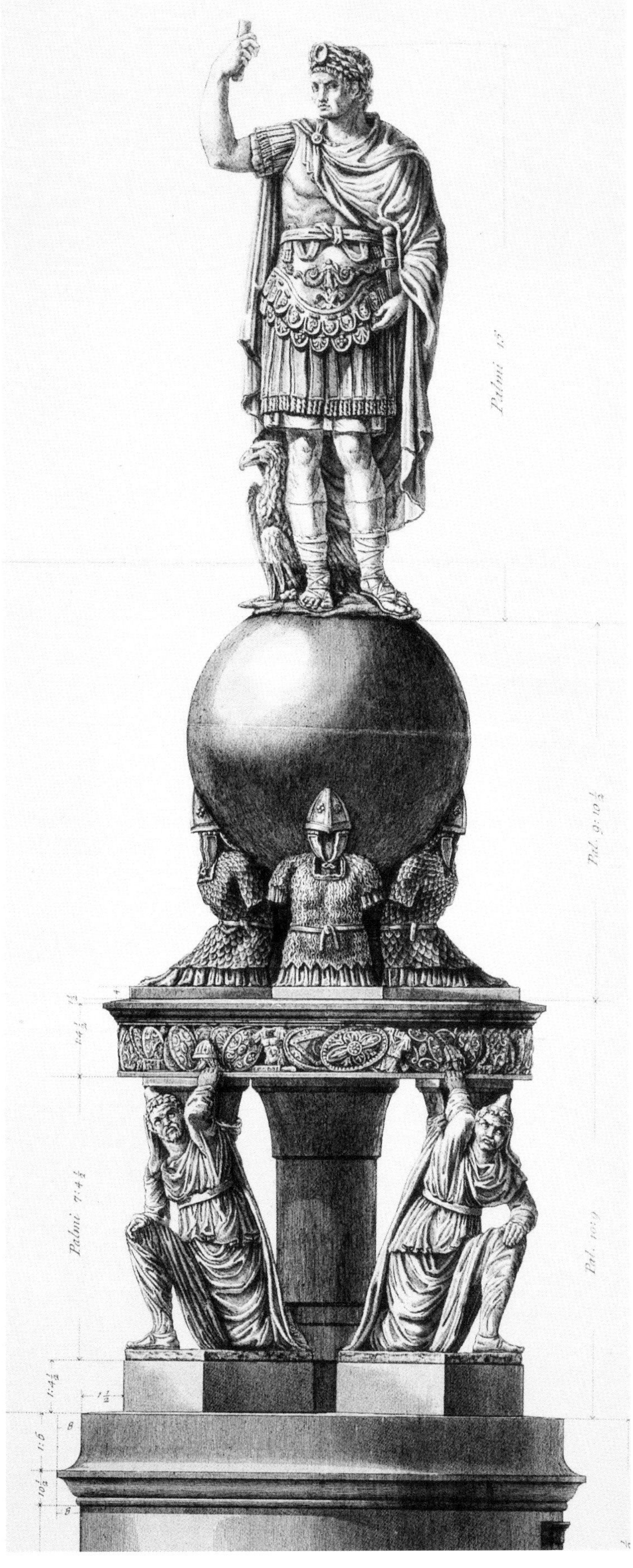

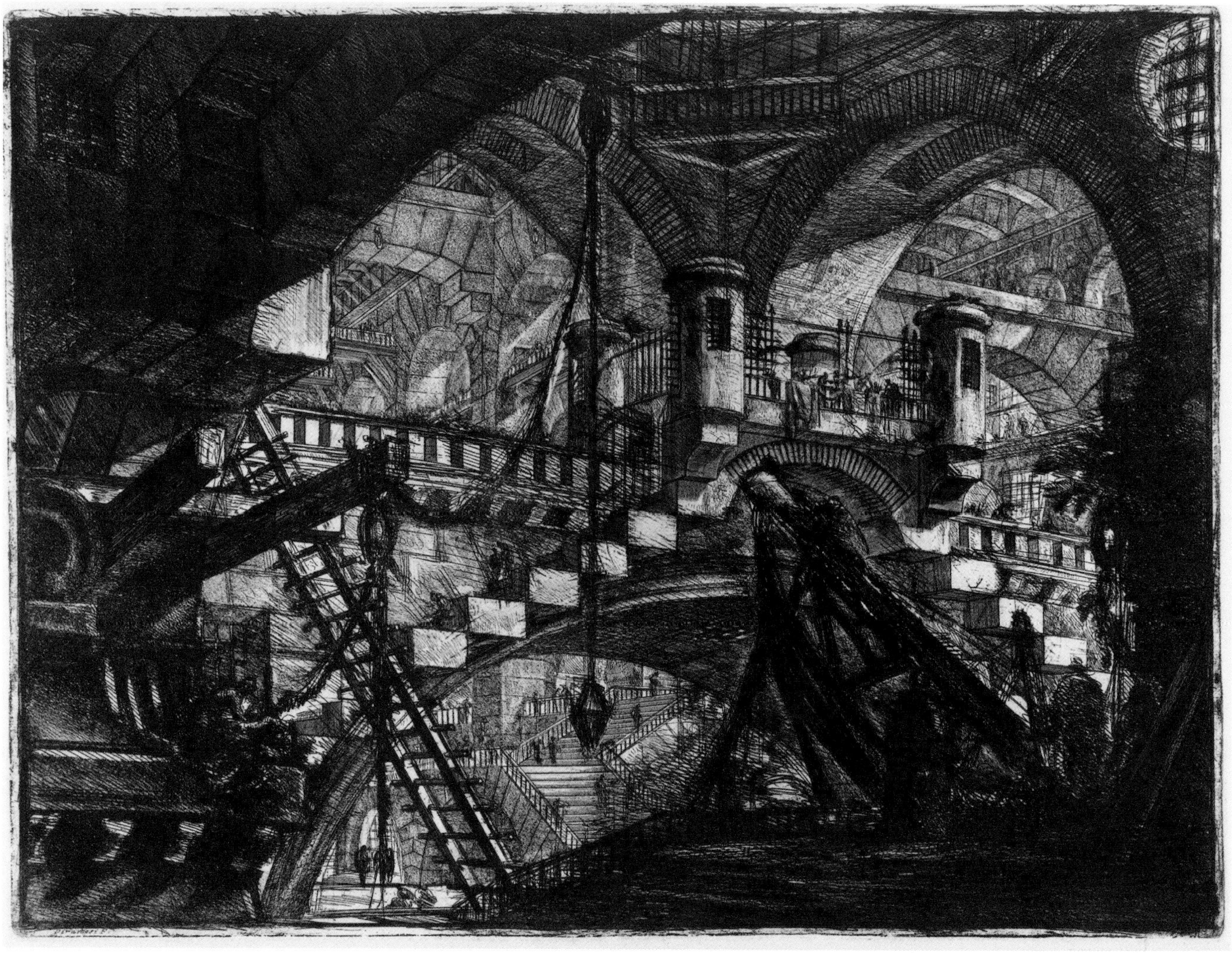

24
Giovanni Battista Piranesi (1720–1778), *The Arch with a Shell Ornament*, from *Imaginary Prisons*, etching, engraving, and drypoint, about 1765–75, purchased through the Mrs. Harvey P. Hood W'18 Fund; PR.995.8

Roman buildings. As a result, his extraordinary ability to both document and recreate the heritage of the past inspired generations of writers and artists to reassess the magnificence of the classical world.

THE GRAND TOUR

When Johann Wolfgang Goethe (1749–1832) arrived in Rome in early November 1786, he immediately compared his first impressions of the city's monuments to his recollections of Piranesi's images, which his father had acquired during a trip to Italy and had displayed in their house in Germany. Throughout the diary entries in his *Italian Journey*, Goethe referred to the printed images of sites and objects that had served as important visual resources for learning about Roman civilization before his trip and that would continue to be useful in the future as mementos. Yet, in spite of the increasing availability of high-quality reproductions in the eighteenth century, a trip to Italy with Rome as its central goal—called the "Grand Tour"—became an essential ingredient in the proper education of many upper-class Europeans. As Anthony Ashley Cooper, earl of Shaftesbury (1671–1713), advocated in 1711, people must form "[their] Judgment of Arts . . . upon right Models of Perfection. If [they] travel to Rome, [they] inquire which are the truest Pieces of Architecture, the best Remains of Statues . . . . However antiquated, rough, or dismal they may appear, at first sight, [they must] resolve to view them over and over, till [they] have brought themselves to relish them, and find their hidden Graces and Perfections."[14]

Even though eighteenth-century trips to Rome were a well-established tradition in many countries, the majority of those embarking on the Grand Tour were from England. Guided by early published accounts and traveling according to standard itineraries, sometimes lasting for years, English tourists sought to reconstruct Roman antiquity by visiting the sites described in ancient literature and using surviving sculptures to elucidate events in classical history. As Joseph Addison (1672–1719) noted in his *Remarks on Several Parts of Italy*, first published in 1705, the tour served as a means to steep oneself in the glories that the English sought to recreate. Eventually, like-minded individuals who had traveled to Rome and who supported and sponsored antiquarian studies formed a few English societies in London. These groups also financed expeditions to Greece and Asia Minor, but throughout this period the main focus of the Grand Tour remained Rome.

One visitor to the city in early 1729 was Sir Robert Throckmorton (1702–1791), then fourth baronet of Coughton Court, Warwick, who was living in France due to his family's continuing allegiance to Catholicism. While little is known about his specific activities and movements around Rome from mid-January to late April, he would return to England and eventually acquire in 1754 two volumes of Piranesi's prints (Figure 25), now in the collection of the Hood Museum of Art.[15] Throckmorton's acquisition of these publications so soon after their appearance was probably inspired by his own vivid recollections, as well as a recognition of the prestige that etchings and engravings had attained by the middle of the eighteenth century. By this time, prints were no longer seen merely as illustrations for guidebooks and souvenirs; instead, their large size and impressive visual impact made them desirable objects for prominent display.

25
(following pages)
Giovanni Battista Piranesi (1720–1778), *The Campo Vaccino*, etching, from *The Magnificences of Rome*, published 1752, Hood Museum of Art, Dartmouth College; PR.977.24.19

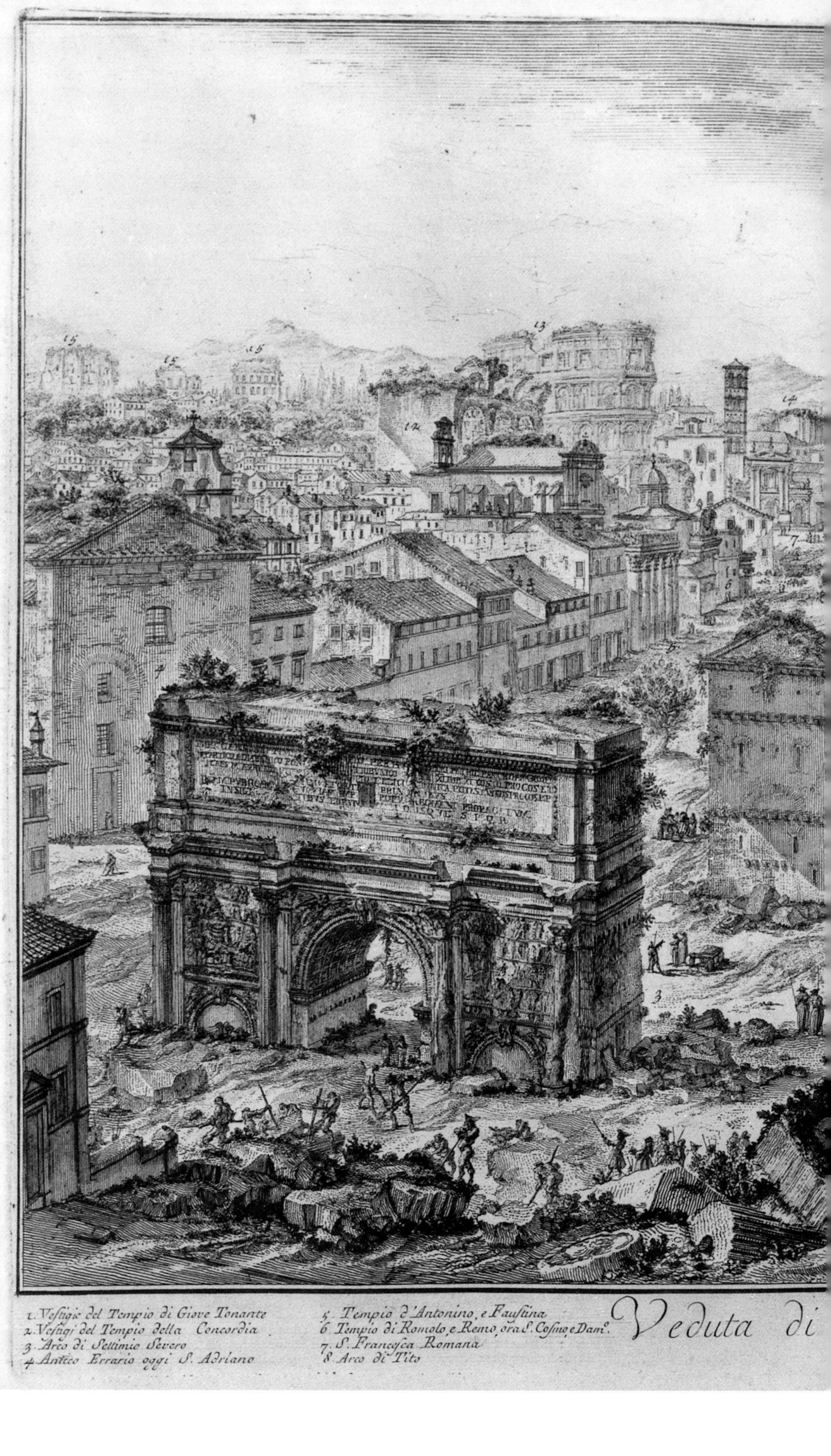
1. Vestigie del Tempio di Giove Tonante
2. Vestigi del Tempio della Concordia
3. Arco di Settimio Severo
4 Antico Errario oggi S. Adriano
5. Tempio d'Antonino, e Faustina
6 Tempio di Romolo, e Remo, ora S. Cosmo e Dam.°
7. S. Francesca Romana
8 Arco di Tito
Veduta di

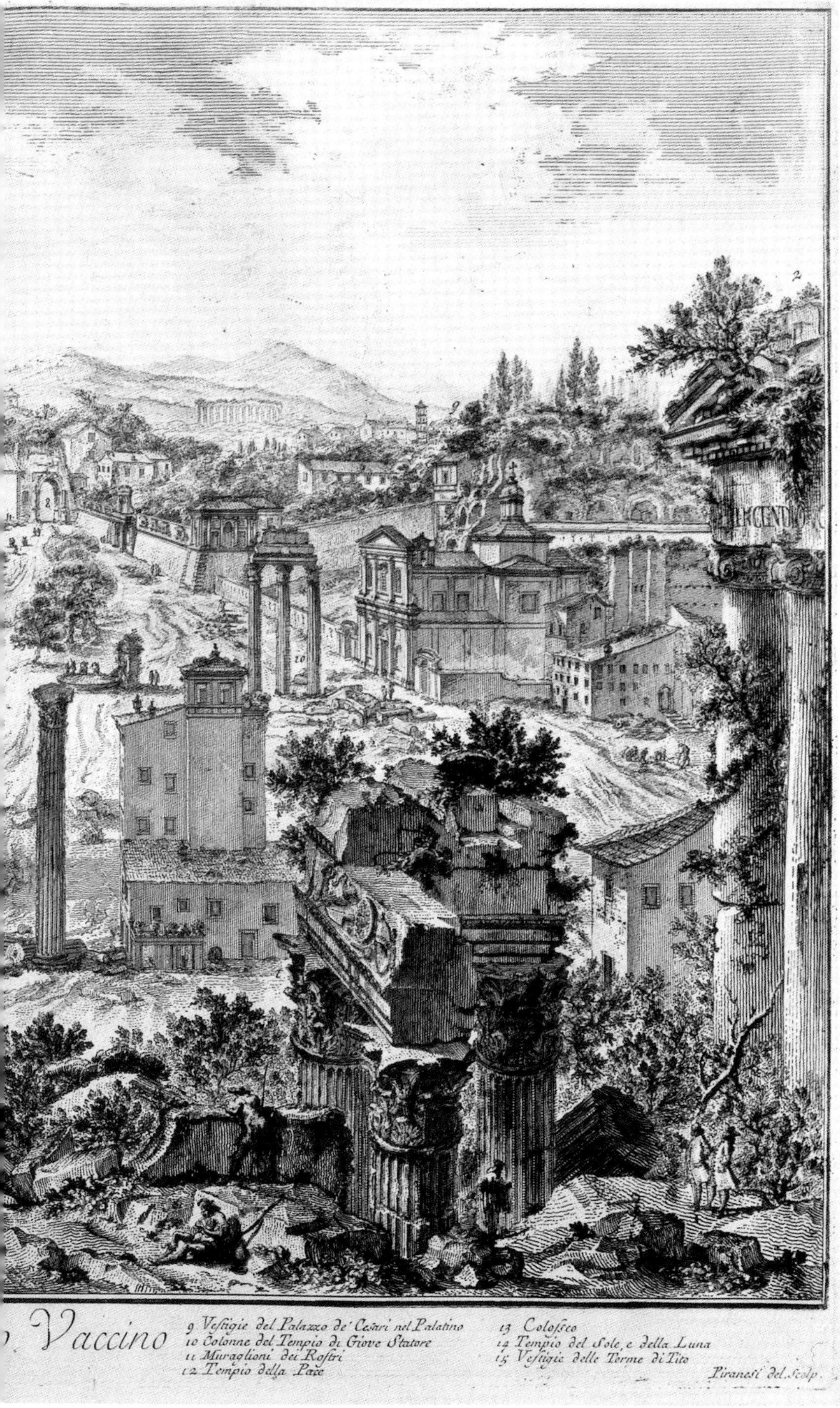

Vaccino
9 Vestigie del Palazzo de' Cesari nel Palatino
10 Colonne del Tempio di Giove Statore
11 Muraglioni dei Rostri
12 Tempio della Pace
13 Colosseo
14 Tempio del Sole, e della Luna
15 Vestigie delle Terme di Tito
Piranesi del. Scolp.

The prestige associated with owning such prized items was considerable, but even more highly regarded were beautifully carved replicas of famous antiquities. In the case of the approximately half-size reproduction of the ancient *Hermaphrodite* by Laurent Delvaux (1696–1778; Figure 26), the demand for such works of art has been well documented. Sometime around the beginning of the seventeenth century, the original *Hermaphrodite* was discovered near the Baths of Diocletian. According to the account books of Cardinal Scipione Borghese (about 1576–1633), Gian Lorenzo Bernini was paid in 1620 for restoring the antique marble and for making "a mattress" for the statue. Thereafter, from the time it was put on display in the newly constructed Villa Borghese along with other objects in the cardinal's famous collection of antiquities, the sleeping figure and its bed were one of the most admired sculptures in Rome (until, that is, it was moved to Paris sometime between 1808 and 1811). Bernini's addition of a realistic mattress was criticized in the late eighteenth century by some observers, yet it clearly reflected the artist's attitude toward classical art. In his mind, the sculpture was not something merely to be revered, and embellishments to it were a sign of the marble's contemporary significance. Although modern restorations to other ancient statues were frequently recognized, Bernini's intervention was consistently acknowledged and frequently celebrated.

Bronze, marble, terracotta, and plaster copies were made of the sculpture as early as the middle of the seventeenth century, most of which were smaller in scale than the original. At least three marble, half-size replicas were made by Delvaux around 1730, one of them signed and dated in Rome in that year. This one was commissioned by Lord John Russel, fourth duke of Bedford (1710–1771), who visited the Eternal City from late November 1730 to February 1731. It was actually the architect who was planning the duke's Palladian-style residence in England that recommended acquiring five sculptures from Delvaux, all closely derived from well-known antique sculptures. The architect thought that these statues would be appropriate furnishings for the classical design of the new mansion at Woburn Abbey (which was never realized).

In addition to prints and sculptures that reproduced antiquities, travelers returning from the Grand Tour sent back paintings, furniture, and other decorative arts objects, including portraits, urban views, landscapes, and other souvenirs of sites and artifacts that recalled the splendors of a lost ancient world and various artistic interpretations of its heritage (from Raphael to Piranesi). Through this type of patronage, tourists helped to record the magnificence of the past and to promote its continuing relevance to contemporary culture. The survival of certain antique works of art and the revival of specific aesthetic ideals and principles associated with them established the legacy of the classical tradition throughout Europe in the seventeenth and eighteenth centuries.

EPILOGUE

Ironically, the dissemination of classicism throughout Europe in the late eighteenth century made art essentially independent from the ancient traditions represented by Rome. As one scholar has recently observed, this phenomenon marked the beginning of the end of Roman preeminence in painting,

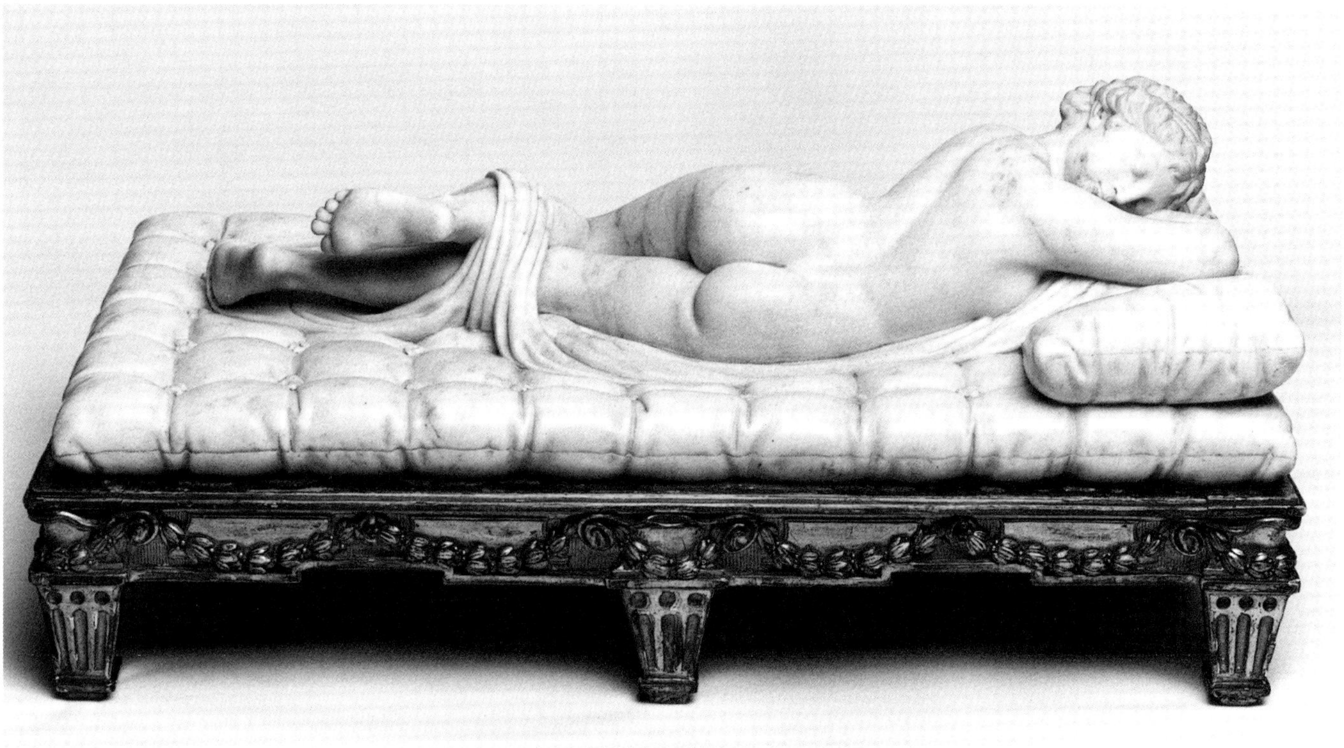

26
Laurent Delvaux (1696–1778), after unknown, Roman, and Gian Lorenzo Bernini (1598–1680), *Hermaphrodite*, marble, after 1730, collection of David P. Southwell, Tuck 1988, and Barbara Dau Southwell, Class of 1978

sculpture, and architecture in the European imagination.[16] Even before the emergence of this trend, however, the absolute authority of the ancients was being questioned throughout the Baroque era. While many artists and critics believed that greatness and perfection could only be achieved by copying antique examples, a few dissenting voices argued against classicism becoming a restrictive dogma. Gradually, new aesthetic approaches appeared as the challenges to accepted norms increased.

One of the first artists to caution against excessive dependence on antiquity at the risk of inhibiting creativity was Peter Paul Rubens, whose archeological knowledge was rivaled only by that of Nicolas Poussin of the next generation of European painters. Sometime in the early seventeenth century, Rubens wrote an elegant Latin treatise entitled "Concerning the Imitation of Antique Statues," in which he wrote that "To some painters the imitation of antique statues has been extremely useful, and to others pernicious, even to the ruin of their art."[17] Rubens feared that slavish adherence to artificial models would restrict innovation, and he therefore stressed inspiration over imitation, and visual persuasion over intellectual vision.

Others were concerned with the development of the academic tradition since the end of the sixteenth century, which had consistently established classical models as the fundamental sources for young artists to emulate. These institutions believed that ancient rules and practices would guide painters, sculptors, and architects to perfection in their work, as well as provide them with criteria for understanding and appreciating art. An example of a prominent painter who did not adhere to this tradition was Rembrandt van Rijn (1606–1669), who was ridiculed by some of his contemporaries for his resistance to these doctrines. Joachim van Sandrart (1606–1688), who was active in the academies in both Augsburg and Nuremberg, acknowledged that Rembrandt had not ignored the "observation of nature," nor was he sparing in his "industry and constant application" of his art. However, he deplored the fact that the well-known painter "had never visited Italy or other places where he might have studied antiquities and art theory, and since he could only read Dutch—and even that badly—he could find little help in books. Thus he never changed his ways and did not hesitate to contradict our theories on . . . the usefulness of classical statues . . . . And he also argued against the academies that are so very necessary to our profession, reasoning that one should only, and exclusively, follow nature and no other rules."[18]

Ultimately, Rubens' and Rembrandt's emphasis on the effects of light, color, and space over design, decorum, and historical accuracy was adopted as the essential basis of painting by the majority of nineteenth-century artists, largely signaling the end of the classical tradition in the arts.

Notes

1. *Delle lettere*, ed. Pietro Petracci (Venice: G. B. Ciotti, 1604), cited in Luigi Spezzaferro, "La Roma di Sisto V," in *Storia dell'arte italiana: momenti di architettura*, 12 vols. (Turin: Giulio Einaudi editore, 1983), 12:367–68.

2. Giovanni Battista Armenini, *De' veri precetti della pittura* (Ravenna: Francesco Tebaldini, 1587), 61.

3. Before systematic excavations were undertaken at Herculaneum and Pompeii in the eighteenth century, there were relatively few known examples of antique painting. As Karl van Mander (1548–1606) noted at the beginning of the seventeenth century, "The artful, noble works of the celebrated painters of the earlier ages that we call the antique have long since been cruelly destroyed by the teeth of time, and to man's knowledge are nowhere to be seen. They would not only have been wrested from our eyes, but also from our thoughts and minds, such that we would no longer be able to describe them had not the heavenly art of writing preserved and kept them for us in immortal fame" (*Het schilder-boeck* . . . [Haarlem: Paschier van Wesbvach, 1604], 60r).

4. Abbé (Gabriel François) Coyer, *Voyages d'Italie et de Hollande*, 2 vols. (Paris: Veuve Duchesne, 1775), 1:265, cited in Francis Haskell and Nicholas Penny, *Taste and the Antique: The Lure of Classical Sculpture, 1500–1900* (New Haven: Yale University Press, 1981), 164.

5. Filippo Baldinucci, *Cominciamento e progresso dell'arte dell'intagliare in rame* (Florence: Pietro Matini, 1686), 156, cited in Francesca Consagra, "The Marketing of Pietro Testa's 'Poetic Inventions,'" in Elizabeth Cropper, ed., *Pietro Testa, 1612–1650: Prints and Drawings* (Philadelphia: Philadelphia Museum of Art, 1990), lxxxvii.

6. James Kennedy, *A Description of the Antiquities and Curiosities in Wilton House* (Salisbury: E. Easton, 1769), iv.

7. For Bernini's comment, recorded by an eyewitness in 1665, see Paul Fréart de Chantelou, *Diary of Cavaliere Bernini's Visit to France*, ed. Anthony Blunt et al. (Princeton: Princeton University Press, 1985), 80. Cf. also the contemporary debate in the French Academy in 1668 over Poussin's "servile" study of ancient art and his aesthetic ideals, published in English in Elizabeth Holt, ed., *Literary Sources of Art History: An Anthology of Texts from Theophilus to Goethe* (Princeton: Princeton University Press, 1947), 388–94.

8. Alfred Peltzer, ed., *Joachim von Sandrarts Accademie der Bau-, Bild- und Mahlerey-Kunste von 1675: Leben der beruhmten Maler, Bildhauer und Baumeister* [1675–79] (Munich: G. Hirth's Verlag, 1925), 184. See also the comment made by a British artist visiting Tivoli in 1758, who noted that the area "has been ye only school where [one of the] most celebrated painters Claude . . . studied" (cited in Michael Clarke and Nicholas Penny, eds., *The Arrogant Connoisseur, Richard Payne Knight, 1751–1824* [Manchester: Manchester University Press, 1982], 60).

9. Vatican City, Biblioteca Apostolica, Cod. Ferraioli, ms. 415, fol. 25v, cited in Hanns Gross, *Rome in the Age of Enlightenment: The Post-Tridentine Syndrome and the Ancient Regime* (Cambridge and New York: Cambridge University Press, 1990), 311.

10. Jonathan Richardson, Senior and Junior, *An Account of Some of the Statues, Bas-Reliefs, Drawings and Pictures in Italy, etc. with Remarks* (London: J. Knapton, 1722), cited in Haskell and Penny, *Taste and the Antique*, 99.

11. For an interesting reference to the illustrations in Winckelmann's publication, see his unpublished letter sent from Rome on 6 November 1762 (Dartmouth College Library, Manuscript Ticknor 762606/.1).

12. For a discussion of the specific sources, see Anne L. Poulet and Guilhem Scherf, *Clodion, 1738–1814* (Paris: Réunion des Musée Nationaux, 1992), no. 23, 157–61.

13. Piranesi's opinions are recorded in his "Osservazioni sulla lettera a Mariette" of 1765, republished in John Wilton-Ely, ed., *The Polemical Works* (Farnborough, Hants: Gregg, 1972), 15ff.

14. *Characteristics of Men, Manners, Opinions, Times*, 3 vols. (London: John Darby, 1711), 1:338, cited in Rudolf and Margot Wittkower, *Born Under Saturn; The Character and Conduct of Artists: A Documented History from Antiquity to the French Revolution* (New York and London: W. W. Norton and Company, 1969), 52.

15. For further documentation on Throckmorton's acquisition, see Richard Rand and John Varriano, *Two Views of Italy: Master Prints by Canaletto and Piranesi* (Hanover, N.H.: Hood Museum of Art, Dartmouth College, 1995), 21–23.

16. Christopher M. S. Johns, "The Entrepôt of Europe: Rome in the Eighteenth Century," in *Art in Rome in the Eighteenth Century*, eds. Edgar Peter Bowron and Joseph J. Rishel (Philadelphia: Philadelphia Museum of Art, 2000), 40.

17. First published in English in Roger de Piles, *The Principles of Painting* (London: J. Osborn, 1743), 86.

18. *Joachim von Sandrarts Accademie der Bau-, Bild- und Mahlerey-Kunste von 1675*, 202, cited in English in Wittkower, *Born Under Saturn*, 51.

Checklist of the Exhibition

VIEWS, MONUMENTS, AND RUINS

Michael Wolgemut, German, 1434/37–1519, and workshop
View of Rome
Woodcut
In Hartmann Schedel, German, 1440–1514
Liber chronicarum (Nuremberg: Anton Koberger, 1493), folios 57v–58r
Printed volume
Book closed: 47.3 x 32.6 x 5.8 cm
Collection of Dartmouth College Library
Figures 1a–b

Egidius Sadeler II, Flemish, about 1570–1629, after Etienne Dupèrac, French, about 1525–1601
View of the Pantheon, 1606
Engraving
Sheet: 18.4 x 30.5 cm; plate: 15.9 x 26.7 cm
Gift of the Estate of Professor Harry E. Burton, Class of 1908H; PR.945.57.5

Egidius Sadeler II, Flemish, about 1570–1629, after Etienne Dupèrac, French, about 1525–1601
View of the Arch of Constantine, 1606
Engraving
Sheet: 23.35 x 34.9 cm; plate: 16 x 27.4 cm
Gift of the Estate of Professor Harry E. Burton, Class of 1908H; PR.945.57.3

Giovanni Battista Piranesi, Italian, 1720–1778
The Forum of Augustus from *The Magnificences of Rome*, published 1752
Etching
Sheet: 37.5 x 52.7 cm; plate: 13.4 x 27.7 cm
Hood Museum of Art, Dartmouth College; PR.977.24.83

Giovanni Battista Piranesi, Italian, 1720–1778
The Arch of Constantine from *The Magnificences of Rome*, published 1752
Etching
Sheet: 37.5 x 52.7 cm; plate: 12.9 x 26.2 cm
Hood Museum of Art, Dartmouth College; PR.977.24.91

Jean-Claude Richard, Abbé de Saint Non, French, 1727–1791, after Jean Baptiste Le Prince, French, 1734–1781
Ruins along the Via Appia, 1756
Etching
Sheet: 27.15 x 23.5 cm (trimmed to platemark)
Gift of Robert Dance, Class of 1977; PR.997.15.2

Giovanni Battista Piranesi, Italian, 1720–1778
The Campo Vaccino from *The Magnificences of Rome*, published 1752
Etching
Sheet: 52.7 x 69.9 cm; plate: 40.8 x 54.5 cm
Hood Museum of Art, Dartmouth College; PR.977.24.19
Figure 25

Giovanni Battista Piranesi, Italian, 1720–1778
View of Trajan's Column from *The Magnificences of Rome*, published 1752
Etching
Sheet: 70.4 x 52.7 cm; plate: 54.4 x 40.7 cm
Hood Museum of Art, Dartmouth College; PR.977.24.18

Giovanni Battista Piranesi, Italian, 1720–1778
View of the Principal Elevation of the Antonine Column, about 1776
Etching
Six sheets (overall): 315 x 83.5 cm; plates: (1) 47.63 x 47.82; (2) 50.8 x 47.82; (3) 52.9 x 47.82; (4) 53.66 x 47.82; (5) 55.25 x 47.82; (6) 47 x 47.82 cm
Hood Museum of Art, Dartmouth College; PR.967.130.28

COLLECTING AND STUDYING ANTIQUITIES

Unknown, Roman, second century CE
Sarcophagus Fragment: Eros with Nereids and Tritons, about 140–160 CE
Marble
47 x 120 x 10.2 cm
Acquisitions Fund, Hood Museum of Art; S.977.21
Figure 17

Cristoforo di Geremia, Italian, fifteenth century (active 1456–76)
Constantine the Great, 1468
Bronze
Diameter: 7 cm
Collection of Roger Arvid Anderson, Class of 1968; EL.S.993.19.54

Unknown, Italian, late fifteenth century
Scipio Africanus (Bust of a Soldier in a Plumed Helmet), late fifteenth century
Bronze
7.4 x 5.9 cm
Collection of Roger Arvid Anderson, Class of 1968; EL.S.993.19.117

Unknown, Italian, late fifteenth or early sixteenth century
Timeter after the Antique
Bronze
3.9 x 5.4 cm
Collection of Roger Arvid Anderson, Class of 1968; EL.S.998.42.12

Master IO.F.F., northern Italian, active about 1500
The Judgement of Paris, about 1500
Bronze
Diameter: 5.5 cm
Collection of Roger Arvid Anderson, Class of 1968; EL.S.993.19.20

Master IO.F.F., northern Italian, active about 1500
Ariadne on Naxos, about 1500
Bronze
Diameter: 4.8 cm
Collection of Roger Arvid Anderson, Class of 1968; EL.S.993.19.16

Unknown, Italian
Apollo and Marsyas, about 1500
Bronze
8 x 6 cm
Collection of Roger Arvid Anderson, Class of 1968; EL.S.993.19.69

Medallist of the Roman Emperors
Marcus Croto (reverse), about 1500
Diameter: 6.35 cm
Collection of Roger Arvid Anderson, Class of 1968; EL.S.2000.10

Unknown, northern Italian, sixteenth century, after Cristoforo Foppa, called Caradosso, Italian, about 1452–1526/27
Satyr and Nymph, mid-sixteenth century
Bronze
Diameter: 17.3 cm
Collection of Roger Arvid Anderson, Class of 1968; EL.S.988.21.1

Unknown, Roman, sixteenth century (?)
Hercules
Bronze
11.43 x 10.16 cm
Collection of Roger Arvid Anderson, Class of 1968; EL.S.998.42.7

Attributed to Andrea Sabbatini, Italian, about 1484–1530
Study of a Sculpture of a Goddess, early sixteenth century
Pen and ink and wash
Sheet: 27 x 17.46 cm
Purchased through the Julia L. Whittier Fund; D.947.33

Andrea Palladio, Italian, 1508–1580, and workshop
Pantheon
Woodcut
In Andrea Palladio
I quattro libri dell'architettura . . .
(Venice: D. de' Franceschi, 1570), book 4, pages 76–77
Printed volume
Book closed: 30.4 x 21.2 x 2.5 cm
Collection of Dartmouth College Library

Hendrik Goltzius, Dutch, 1558–1617
The Emperor Commodus as Hercules, about 1591–92; printed 1617
Engraving
Sheet: 41.9 x 30.3 cm; plate: 41.1 x 29.8 cm
Purchased through the Jean and Adolph Weil Jr. 1935 Fund; PR.999.37
Figure 12

Francesco Villamena, Italian, 1566–1624
Portrait of Giovanni Alto, Antiquarian, 1623
Engraving with red and black chalk, working proof
Sheet: 38.3 x 52.5 cm; plate: 37.7 x 52.2 cm
Purchased through the Class of 1935 Memorial Fund and the Jean and Adolph Weil Jr. 1935 Fund; PR.997.29.2
Figure 15

Pietro Santi Bartoli, Italian, 1635–1700, after unknown, Roman, active second century CE
Roman Sarcophagus Representing Orestes' Revenge
Engraving
In Pietro Santi Bartoli
Admiranda romanarum antiquitatum . . .
(Rome: Domenicus de Rubeis, 1693), plate 52
Printed volume
Book closed: 35.5 x 47.12 x 2.5 cm
Collection of Dartmouth College Library
Figure 16

Nicolas Dorigny, French, 1652/58–1746
The Farnese Hercules, 1704
Engraving
Sheet: 46.35 x 31.43 cm; plate: 34.45 x 23.84 cm
Collection of Robert Dance, Class of 1977

Bernard de Montfaucon, French, 1655–1741
Constantine's Arch at Rome
Engraving
In Bernard de Montfaucon
The supplement to Antiquity explained, and represented in sculptures (London: J. Tonson and J. Watts, 1725), plate 91
Printed volume
Book: 39.25 x 26.4 x 4.5 cm
Collection of Dartmouth College Library

Nicolas Dorigny, French, 1652/58–1746, after Carlo Maratta, Italian, 1625–1713
The Academy of Painting, 1728
Engraving
Sheet: 47 x 32.5 cm; plate: 40.2 x 31 cm
Collection of Robert Dance, Class of 1977
Figure 14

François-André Vincent, French, 1746–1816
Bust of Lucius Junius Brutus (The Capitoline Brutus), 1774
Red chalk and wash
Sheet: 52.1 x 29.5 cm
Purchased through a gift from the Cremer Foundation in memory of J. Theodor Cremer and a gift from John W. Thompson, Class of 1908 and Dorothy M. Litzinger, by exchange; D.988.16
Figure 13

Giovanni Battista Piranesi, Italian, 1720–1778
View of the Principal Elevation of the Column of Trajan, about 1774
Etching
Six sheets (overall): 320.68 x 77.15 cm; plates: (1) 20 x 47.31; (2) 54.93 x 47.31; (3) 53.98 x 47.31; (4) 53.98 x 47.31; (5) 53.66 x 47.31; (6) 19.69 x 47.31 cm
Hood Museum of Art, Dartmouth College; PR.967.130.3
Figures 22–23

IMITATION, INSPIRATION, AND INVENTION

Giorgio Ghisi, Italian, 1520–1582, after Raphael, Italian, 1483–1520
The School of Athens, 1550
Engraving, ii/III
Two sheets (overall): 51.4 x 81.6 cm (trimmed to platemark)
Gift of Jane and W. David Dance, Class of 1940; PR.991.58.1
Figure 8

Enea Vico, Italian, 1523–1567, after Polidoro da Caravaggio, Italian, about 1499–about 1543
"All'antica" Trophies, about 1550
Engraving, i/IV
Two separate sheets: (1) 25.2 x 16.85; 23.2 x 16.7 cm; plates: (1) 24.8 x 16.7; (2) 22.95 x 16.5 cm
Purchased through the Julia L. Whittier Fund; PR.2000.38.3/5

Alessandro Specchi, Italian, 1668–1729, after Donato Bramante, Italian, about 1444–1514
Design for the Drum and Dome of St. Peter's Basilica, 1694
Engraving
Sheet: 51.8 x 38.8 cm; plate: 29.05 x 20.48 cm
Gift of Robert Dance, Class of 1977; PR.993.42.36

Laurent Delvaux, French, 1696–1778, after unknown, Roman, and Gian Lorenzo Bernini, Italian, 1598–1680
Hermaphrodite, after 1730
Marble
70 x 37 x 21 cm
Collection of David P. Southwell, Tuck 1988, and Barbara Dau Southwell, Class of 1978
Figure 26

Giovanni Battista Piranesi, Italian, 1720–1778
Part of a Spacious Port Customary of the Ancient Romans where is Revealed the Inside of a Large Square for Commerce, from *The Magnificences of Rome*, published 1752
Etching
Sheet: 52.1 x 69.9 cm; plate: 39.9 x 54.6 cm
Hood Museum of Art, Dartmouth College; PR.977.25.42

Circle of Giovanni Battista Piranesi, Italian, 1720–1778
Studies of Antique Armor, mid-eighteenth century
Pen ink and sepia wash
Sheet: 25.6 x 42.86 cm
Gift of Mrs. Hersey Egginton in memory of her son, Everett Egginton, Class of 1921; D.954.20.667

REPRESENTING CLASSICAL MYTHOLOGY

Andrea Mantegna, Italian, about 1431–1506
Battle of the Sea Gods (left half), 1470s
Engraving, only state
Sheet: 24.5 x 37.3 cm (trimmed within platemark)
Gift of Jean K. Weil in memory of Adolph Weil Jr., Class of 1935; PR.997.5.85
Figure 6

Niccolò di Forzore Spinelli, called Niccolò Fiorentino, Italian, 1430–about 1514
Mercury (Antonio della Lecia) (reverse), about 1475
Bronze
Diameter: 8.6 cm
Collection of Roger Arvid Anderson, Class of 1968; EL.S.993.19.53

Galeazzo Mondella, called il Moderno, Italian, 1467–1528
Hercules and the Nemean Lion, about 1500
Bronze
7.9 x 6.7 cm
Collection of Roger Arvid Anderson, Class of 1968; EL.S.993.19.70

Galeazzo Mondella, called il Moderno, Italian, 1467–1528
Hercules and the Nemean Lion, about 1500
Bronze
7.5 x 5.5 cm
Collection of Roger Arvid Anderson, Class of 1968; EL.S.993.19.71

Unknown, Italian
Meleager on Horseback, about 1500
Bronze
Diameter: 9.3 cm
Collection of Roger Arvid Anderson, Class of 1968; EL.S.993.19.74

Unknown, Italian
Plaquette of a Miniature Shield, sixteenth century
Bronze
Diameter: 10.2 cm
Collection of Roger Arvid Anderson, Class of 1968; EL.S.998.42.15

Galeazzo Mondella, called il Moderno, Italian, 1467–1528
The Flagellation of Christ, about 1506–09
Gilt bronze
14.3 x 10.7 cm
Collection of Roger Arvid Anderson, Class of 1968; EL.S.995.56.2
Figure 4

Marco Dente, Italian, about 1493–1527, after Marcantonio Raimondi, Italian, about 1470–about 1527, after Raphael, Italian, 1483–1520
The Judgment of Paris, about 1520
Engraving
Sheet: 28.89 x 43.50 cm (trimmed to platemark)
Purchased through the Julia L. Whittier Fund; PR.971.25
Figure 7

Adamo Scultori, Italian, about 1530–1585, after Michelangelo Buonarroti, Italian, 1475–1564
Ignudi, mid-sixteenth century
Engraving
Sheet: (1) 10.9 x 15; (2) 11 x 14.75 cm; plate: (1) 10 x 14; (2) 10 x 14 cm
Collection of Robert Dance, Class of 1977

Giorgio Ghisi, Italian, 1520–1582, after Giovanni Battista Bertani, Italian, about 1515–1576
Hercules Victorious Over the Hydra, about 1558
Engraving
Sheet: 36 x 22 cm; plate: 35 x 21.1 cm
Collection of Robert Dance, Class of 1977

Unknown, Italian
Peter and Paul Healing the Lame Man, about 1560
Gilt silver
14.92 x 21.27 cm
Collection of Roger Arvid Anderson, Class of 1968; EL.S.994.35.83

Andrea Andreani, Italian, 1558/59–1629, after Giuseppe Nicolò Rossigliani, called Vicentino, Italian, active first half of the sixteenth century, after Raphael, Italian, 1483–1520
Hercules Wrestling with the Nemean Lion, late sixteenth century
Chiaroscuro woodcut
Sheet: 24.77 x 19.05 cm
Gift of Dr. F. H. Hirschland; PR.948.66
Figure 2

Claude Michel, called Clodion, French, 1738–1814
The Sacrifice to Cupid, about 1765–70
Marble
26.7 x 30.9 x 2.5 cm
Collection of Roger Arvid Anderson, Class of 1968; EL.S.998.28
Figure 21

Unknown, French, circle of François Boucher, French, 1703–1770
Head of a Faun, about 1775
Red chalk and graphite
Sheet: 34.61 x 27.94 cm
Purchased through the Julia L. Whittier Fund; D.984.3.3

REPRESENTING ANTIQUITY

Marcantonio Raimondi, Italian, about 1470–about 1527, after Raphael, Italian, 1483–1520
Saint Paul Preaching in Athens, about 1517–20
Engraving, only state
Sheet: 26.6 x 35.1 cm (trimmed to platemark)
Purchased through a gift from Stephen and Bonnie Simon and the Esther Simon Charitable Trust; PR.988.26
Figure 9

Marcantonio Raimondi, Italian, about 1470–about 1527, after Raphael, Italian, 1483–1520
Holy Family with Saint John the Baptist, about 1520–25
Engraving
Sheet: 40.6 x 26.8 cm; plate: 40 x 26.65 cm
Purchased through a gift from Stephen and Bonnie Simon and the Esther Simon Charitable Trust; PR.988.27
Figure 10

Giorgio Ghisi, Italian, 1520–1582, after Polidoro Caldara da Caravaggio, Italian, about 1499–about 1543
Caius Marius in Prison, 1560s
Engraving
Sheet: 22 x 29.5 cm; plate: 20.6 x 28.7 cm
Collection of Robert Dance, Class of 1977

Salvator Rosa, Italian, 1615–1673
Democritus in Meditation, 1662
Etching and drypoint, state ii/II
Sheet: 49.9 x 30.9 cm; plate: 45.6 x 27.6 cm
Purchased through the Guernsey Center Moore 1904 Memorial Fund; PR.964.120

Sebastien Bourdon, French, 1616–1671
Clothe the Naked (Vestire nudos), from *Acts of Mercy*, about 1665–70
Etching and engraving, state i/III
Sheet: 43.65 x 58.89 cm
Purchased through the Julia L. Whittier Fund; PR.971.6.4
Figure 19

Gilles Rousselet, French, 1610–1686, after Nicolas Poussin, French, 1594–1665
Eliezer and Rebecca at the Well, 1677
Engraving, only state
Sheet: 45.5 x 64.9 cm; plate: 43 x 64 cm
Purchased through the Guernsey Center Moore 1904 Memorial Fund, the Class of 1935 Memorial Fund, the Mrs. Harvey P. Hood W'18 Fund, and the Julia L. Whittier Fund; PR.997.3.4
Figure 18

Pietro Aquila, Italian, active late seventeenth century (died 1692), after Pietro Berrettini, called Pietro da Cortona, Italian, 1596–1669
Xenophon's Sacrifice to Diana, late seventeenth century
Engraving
Sheet: 49.21 x 75.25 cm; plate: 43.82 x 62.87 cm
Purchased through the Class of 1935 Memorial Fund; PR.2000.42.1

Louis de Boullongne, French, 1654–1733
Alexander and Diogenes, about 1695
Oil on canvas
48 x 56 cm
Purchased through the Mrs. Harvey P. Hood W'18 Fund; P.993.6

Attributed to Francesco Trevisani, Italian, 1656–1746
Alexander and the Wife of Darius, about 1735
Pen and ink, wash, and white heightening
Sheet: 17.5 x 18.4 cm
Gift of Anthony and Lois Blumka; D.993.43.1

CAPRICCI, FANTASIES, AND IDEAL LANDSCAPES

Unknown, Italian, active late fifteenth century
Elephant and Obelisk
Woodcut
In Francesco Colonna, Italian, died 1527
Hypnerotomachia Poliphili (Venice: Aldus Manuntius, 1499)
Printed volume
Book closed: 31.7 x 21.3 x 4.8 cm
Collection of Dartmouth College Library
Figure 11

Claude Lorrain, French, 1600–1682
Landscape with a Shepherd and Shepherdess, about 1636
Oil on canvas
74.0 x 97.2 cm
Purchased through gifts from Peter and Kirsten Bedford and Julia and Richard H. Rush, Class of 1937, and through the Mrs. Harvey P. Hood W'18 Fund, the Guernsey Center Moore 1904 Memorial Fund, and the Merrill and Katherine Beede 1929 Fund, and through gifts by exchange; P.989.21
Figure 20

Giovanni Battista Montano, Italian, 1534–1621
Ideal Temple
Engraving
In Giovanni Battista Montano
Raccolta de tempij . . . (Rome: Calisto, 1638)
Printed volume
Book closed: 25.45 x 34.8 x 1.1 cm
Collection of Dartmouth College Library

Giovanni Antonio Canal, called Canaletto, Italian, 1697–1768
The Portico with the Lantern, about 1740–44
Etching
Sheet: 41.7 x 52.3 cm; plate: 30.3 x 43.8 cm
Gift of Jean K. Weil in memory of Adolph Weil Jr., Class of 1935; PR.997.5.31

Giovanni Antonio Canal, called Canaletto, Italian, 1697–1768
Landscape with Ruined Monuments, about 1740–44
Etching
Sheet 18.0 x 24.8 cm; plate: 14.4 x 21.8 cm
Gift of Jean K. Weil in memory of Adolph Weil Jr., Class of 1935; PR.997.5.50

Jean Le Pautre, French, 1618–1682
Antique fountain
Etching
In Jean Le Pautre
Oeuvres d'architecture de Jean Le Pautre, Architecte, Dessinateur & Graveur du Roi
(Paris: C. A. Jombert, 1751)
Printed volume
Book closed: 34.95 x 23.7 x 4 cm
Collection of Dartmouth College Library

Giovanni Battista Piranesi, Italian, 1720–1778
First Part of Architecture and Perspective Invented and Engraved by Giovanni Battista Piranesi, Venetian Architect among the Salcindio Tiseio Arcadez, from *The Magnificences of Rome*, published 1752
Etching
Sheet: 52.2 x 37.2 cm; plate: 37.5 x 25.2 cm
Hood Museum of Art, Dartmouth College; PR.977.25.23

Giovanni Battista Piranesi, Italian, 1720–1778
Ruins with Skeletons and Shell Forms, from *The Magnificences of Rome*, published 1752
Etching
Sheet 52.4 x 70.5 cm; plate: 39.1 x 54.6 cm
Hood Museum of Art, Dartmouth College; PR.977.25.47

Giovanni Battista Piranesi, Italian, 1720–1778
The Arch with a Shell Ornament, from *Imaginary Prisons*, 1745–50; published 1753
Etching
Sheet: 52.4 x 70.2 cm; plate: 40.4 x 54.3 cm
Hood Museum of Art, Dartmouth College; PR.977.25.55

Giovanni Battista Piranesi, Italian, 1720–1778
The Arch with a Shell Ornament, from *Imaginary Prisons*, about 1765–75
Etching, engraving, and drypoint
Sheet: 44.4 x 58.9 cm; plate: 40.5 x 54.8 cm
Purchased through the Mrs. Harvey P. Hood W'18 Fund; PR.995.8
Figure 24

Bibliography

Addison, Joseph. *Remarks on several parts of Italy, etc., in the years 1701, 1702, 1703*. London: Jacob Tonson, 1705.

Avery, Charles. "Laurent Delvaux's Sculpture at Woburn Abbey." *Apollo* 118, no. 260 n.s. (October 1983): 312–21.

Barkan, Leonard. *Unearthing the Past: Archaeology and Aesthetics in the Making of Renaissance Culture*. New Haven and London: Yale University Press, 1999.

Bartoli, Pietro Santi and Giovanni Pietro Bellori. *Admiranda Romanarum antiquitatum ac veteris sculpturae vestigia . . .* Rome: Dominicus de Rubeis, 1693.

Baxandall, Michael. *Giotto and the Orators: Humanist Observers of Painting in Italy and the Discovery of Pictorial Composition, 1350–1450*. Oxford: Clarendon Press, 1971.

Beneš, Mirka. "Pastoralism in the Roman Baroque Villa and in Claude Lorrain: Myths and Realities of the Roman Campagna." In *Villas and Gardens in Early Modern Italy and France*, eds. Mirka Beneš and Dianne Harris, 88–113. Cambridge and New York: Cambridge University Press, 2001.

Biondo, Flavio. *De Roma triumphante libri decem . . . [et] Romae instaurate libri III . . .* Basel: Froben, 1531.

Blunt, Anthony. *Nicolas Poussin*, 2 vols. New York: Bollingen Foundation, 1967.

Bober, Phyllis Pray and Ruth Rubinstein. *Renaissance Artists and Antique Sculpture: A Handbook of Sources*. London: Harvey Miller; Oxford: Oxford University Press, 1986.

Bold, John with John Reeves. *Wilton House and English Palladianism: Some Wiltshire Houses*. London: Her Majesty's Stationery Office, 1988.

Borea, Evelina and Carlo Gasparri. *L'idea del bello: Viaggio per Roma nel Seicento con Giovan Pietro Bellori*, 2 vols. Exhibition catalogue. Rome: Edizioni De Luca, 2000.

Bowron, Edgar Peters and Joseph J. Rishel. *Art in Rome in the Eighteenth Century*. Exhibition catalogue. Philadelphia: Philadelphia Museum of Art, 2000.

Bracciolini, Poggio. *De varietate fortunae*. Paris: D. Gregorius, 1723; reprinted Bologna: Forni, 1969.

Brandenburg, Hugo. "Meerwesensarkophage und Clipeusmotiv: Beiträge zur Interpretation Römischer Sarkophagreliefs." *Jahrbuch des Deutschen Archäologischen Instituts* 82 (1967): 195–245.

Brummer, Hans Henrik. *The Statue Court in the Vatican Belvedere*. Stockholm: Alquist and Wiksell, 1970.

Buberl, Brigitte, ed. *Roma Antica: Römische Ruinen in der italienischen Kunst des 18. Jahrhunderts*. Munich: Hirmer, 1994.

Campbell, Richard J. and Victor Carlson, eds. *Visions of Antiquity: Neoclassical Figure Drawings*. Exhibition catalogue. Los Angeles: Los Angeles County Museum of Art; Minneapolis: Minneapolis Institute of Arts, 1993.

Colonna, Francesco. *Hypnerotomachia Poliphili: The Strife of Love in a Dream*, trans. Joscelyn Godwin. London: Thames and Hudson, 1999.

Cropper, Elizabeth. "On Beautiful Women, Parmagianino, 'Petrarchismo,' and the Vernacular Style." *The Art Bulletin* 58, no. 3 (September 1976): 374–94.

Dacos, Nicole. "Arte italiana e arte antica." In *Storia dell'arte italiana. Parte prina: materiali e problemi*, ed. Giovanni Previtali, 4 vols., 3:3–68. Turin: Giulio Einaudi editore, 1979.

Denison, Cara D., Myra Nan Rosenfeld, and Stephanie Wiles. *Exploring Rome: Piranesi and His Contemporaries*. Exhibition catalogue. New York: Pierpont Morgan Library; Montréal: Centre Canadien d'Architecture, 1993.

D'Onofrio, Cesare. *Visitiamo Roma nel Quattrocento*. Rome: Romana Società Editrice, 1989.

Fagiolo, Marcello, ed. *Roma e l'antico nell'arte e nella cultura del Cinquecento*. Rome: Istituto della Enciclopedia Italiana, 1985.

Galbraith, David. "Petrarch and the Broken City." In *Antiquity and Its Interpreters*, eds. Alina Payne, Ann Kuttner, and Rebekah Smick, 17–26. Cambridge and New York: Cambridge University Press, 1999.

Giehlow, Karl. "Die Hieroglyphenkunde des Humanismus in der Allegorie der Renaissance." *Jahrbuch der Kunstsammlungen des Allerhöchsten Kaiserhauses* 32 (1915): 1–24.

Goethe, Johann Wolfgang. *Italian Journey*, trans. W. H. Auden and Elizabeth Mayer. Harmondsworth, Middlesex, and New York: Penguin Books, 1987.

Goldschmidt, Adolf. "Das Nachleben der antiken Formen in Mittelalter." *Vorträge der Bibliothek Warburg* (1921–22): 40–50.

Graf, Arturo. *Roma nella memoria e nelle immaginazioni del medio evo*, 2 vols. Turin: Loescher, 1882–83.

Gramaccini, Norberto. *Mirabilia: Das Nachleben antiker Statuen vor der Renaissance*. Mainz: Philipp von Zabern, 1996.

Greene, Thomas. *The Light in Troy: Imitation and Discovery in Renaissance Poetry*. New Haven and London: Yale University Press, 1982.

Harcourt, Glenn, ed. *Hendrick Goltzius and the Classical Tradition*. Exhibition catalogue. Los Angeles: Fisher Gallery, University of Southern California, 1992.

Haskell, Francis. *Patrons and Painters: A Study in Relations between Italian Art and Society in the Age of the Baroque*. New York: Alfred A. Knopf, Inc., 1963.

Haskell, Francis and Nicholas Penny. *Taste and the Antique: The Lure of Classical Sculpture 1500–1900*. New Haven and London: Yale University Press, 1981.

Heckscher, William S. "Relics of Pagan Antiquity in Medieval Settings." *Journal of the Warburg Institute* 1, no. 3 (1938): 204–20.

Huebener, Paul Gustav. *Le statue di Roma: Grundlagen für eine Geschichte der antiken Monumente in der Renaissance*. Leipzig: Klinkhardt and Biermann, 1912.

Ingamells, John. *A Dictionary of British and Irish Travelers in Italy, 1701–1800*. New Haven and London: Yale University Press, 1997.

Iverson, Erik. *The Obelisks of Rome*, 2 vols. Copenhagen: Gad, 1968.

Jacks, Philip. *The Antiquarian and the Myth of Antiquity: The Origins of Rome in Renaissance Thought*. Cambridge: Cambridge University Press, 1993.

Jacobs, Alain. *Laurent Delvaux, 1696–1778*. Paris: ARTHENA, 1999.

Joyce, Hetty. "Grasping at Shadows: Ancient Paintings in Renaissance and Baroque Rome." *The Art Bulletin* 74, no. 2 (June 1992): 219–46.

Judson, J. Richard. "Observations on the Use of the Antique in Sixteenth-Century Netherlandish Art." In *Rubens and His World*, ed. Roger Adolf d'Hulst, 49–59. Antwerp: Het Gulden Cabinet, 1985.

Kennedy, I. G. "Claude and Architecture." *Journal of the Warburg and Courtauld Institutes* 35 (1972): 260–83.

Lauro, Giacomo. *Antiquae urbis splendor . . .* Rome: [s.n.], 1612–28 [i.e., 1637].

Levenson, Jay A., Konrad Oberhuber, and Jacquelyn L. Sheehan. *Early Italian Engravings from the National Gallery of Art*. Washington, D.C.: National Gallery of Art, 1973.

Mazzocco, Angelo. "Petrarch, Poggio, and Biondo: Humanism's Foremost Interpreters of Roman Ruins." In *Francis Petrarch Six Centuries Later: A Symposium*, ed. Aldo Scaglione. Chapel Hill, N.C.: Department of Romance Languages, University of North Carolina, 1975

Momigliano, Arnaldo. "Ancient History and the Antiquarian." *Journal of the Warburg and Courtauld Institutes* 13 (1950): 285–315.

Mommsen, Theodor. *Medieval and Renaissance Studies*, ed. Eugene F. Rice Jr. Ithaca, N.Y.: Cornell University Press, 1959.

Montfaucon, Bernard de. *Antiquity explained, and represented in sculptures*, trans. David Humphreys, 5 vols. London: J. Tonson and J. Watts, 1721–22.

Montfaucon, Bernard de. *The Supplement to Antiquity explained, and represented in sculptures*, trans. David Humphreys, 5 vols. London: J. Tonson and J. Watts, 1725.

Nichols, Lawrence W. *Piranesi at Dartmouth: Etchings by Giovanni Battista Piranesi in the Dartmouth College Collections*. Hanover, N.H.: Dartmouth College, 1976.

Panofsky, Erwin. *Renaissance and Renascences in Western Art*. Stockholm: Almquist and Wiksell, 1960.

Panofsky, Erwin and Fritz Saxl. "Classical Mythology in Medieval Art." *Metropolitan Museum Studies* 4, no. 2 (1933): 228–80.

Pater, Walter. *Selected Works*, ed. Richard Aldington. New York: Duell, Sloan, and Pearce, 1948.

Penny, Nicholas. "Antique Sculpture in the Work of Piranesi." In *Piranesi tra Venezia e l'Europa*, ed. Alessandro Bettagno, 45–50. Florence: Leo S. Olschki, 1983.

Petrarch, Francesco. *Rerum familiarium libri I–VIII*, trans. Aldo S. Bernardo. Albany, N.Y.: State University of New York Press, 1975.

Pevesner, Nikolaus. *Academies of Art Past and Present*. Cambridge: Cambridge University Press, 1940.

Ramsey, Paul A., ed. *Rome in the Renaissance: The City and the Myth*. Binghamton, N.Y.: MRTS, 1982.

Rand, Richard and John Varriano. *Two Views of Italy: Master Prints by Canaletto and Piranesi*. Exhibition catalogue. Hanover, N.H.: Hood Museum of Art, Dartmouth College, 1995.

Richardson, Jonathan, Senior and Junior. *An Account of Some of the Statues, Bas-Reliefs, Drawings, and Pictures in Italy, etc., with Remarks*. London: J. Knapton, 1722.

Robison, Andrew. *Piranesi; Early Architectural Fantasies: A Catalogue Raisonné of the Etchings*. Washington: National Gallery of Art; Chicago and London: University of Chicago Press, 1986.

Rosenberg, Pierre and Louis-Antoine Prat. *Nicolas Poussin, 1594–1665*. Exhibition catalogue. Paris: Réunion des Musées Nationaux, 1994.

Roethlisberger, Marcel. "Claude Lorrain: Some New Perspectives." *Studies in the History of Art* 14 (1984): 47–65.

Schudt, Ludwig. *Italienreisen im 17. und 18. Jahrhundert*. Vienna and Munich: Anton Schroll and Co., 1959

Settis, Salvatore, ed. *Memoria dell'antico nell'arte italiana*, 3 vols. Turin: Einaudi, 1986.

Seznec, Jean. *The Survival of the Pagan Gods: The Mythological Tradition and Its Place in Renaissance Humanism and Art*, trans. Barbara Sessions. New York: Pantheon, 1953.

Springer, Anton. "Das Nachleben der Antike im Mittelalter." In *Bilder aus der neueren Kunstgeschichte*, 2 vols. 2nd ed. Bonn: A. Marcus, 1886.

Stechow, Wolfgang. *Rubens and the Classical Tradition*. Cambridge, Mass.: Harvard University Press, 1968.

Stinger, Charles. *The Renaissance in Rome*. Bloomington, Ind.: Indiana University Press, 1985.

Thode, Henry. *Die Antiken in den Stichen Marcantons, Agostino Venezianos und Marco Dentis*. Leipzig: Seeman, 1881.

Thuiller, Jacques. *Sébastien Bourdon, 1616–1671: catalogue critique et chronologique de l'oeuvre complet*. Exhibition catalogue. Paris: Réunion des Musées Nationaux; Montpelier: Musée Fabre; Strasbourg: Musées de Strasbourg, 2000.

Thurber, T. Barton. "Problems of Identification and Identity in Francesco Villamena's Engraved Portrait of Giovanni Alto of 1623." *Word & Image*. Forthcoming.

Turner, Jane, ed. *The Dictionary of Art*, 34 vols., *passim*. New York: Grove's Dictionaries, 1996.

Vermeule, Cornelius. "Classical Archaeology and French Painting in the Seventeenth Century." *Bulletin of the Museum of Fine Arts, Boston* 74, no. 370 (1976): 94–109.

Von Salis, Arnold. *Antike und Renaissance: Über Nachleben und Weiterwirken der alten in der neueren Kunst*. Erlenbach and Zurich: E. Rentsch, 1947.

Warburg, Aby. *Gesammelte Schriften*. Leipzig and Berlin: B. G. Teubner, 1932.

Weiss, Roberto. *The Renaissance Discovery of Classical Antiquity*. 2nd ed. Oxford: Basil Blackwell, 1988.

Wilberding, Erick. "History and Prophecy: Selected Problems in the Religious Paintings of Nicolas Poussin." Ph.D. dissertation. Institute of Fine Arts, New York University, 1997.

Wilton, Andrew and Illaria Bignamini, eds. *The Grand Tour: The Lure of Italy in the Eighteenth Century*. London: Tate Gallery Publishing, 1996.

Winckelmann, Johann Joachim. *The History of Ancient Art*, trans. G. Henry Lodge, 4 vols. New York: F. Ungar, 1968–69.

Winner, Matthias. "'. . . una certa idea.' Maratta zitiert einen Raffaels in einer Zeichnung." In *Der Künstler über sich in seinem Werk: Internationales Symposium der Bibliotheca Hertziana Rom 1989*, ed. Matthias Winner. Weinheim: VCH, Acta Humaniora, 1992.

Zerner, Henry. "Ghisi e la gravure maniériste à Mantoue." *L'Oeil* 13, no. 88 (1962): 26–32; 76.

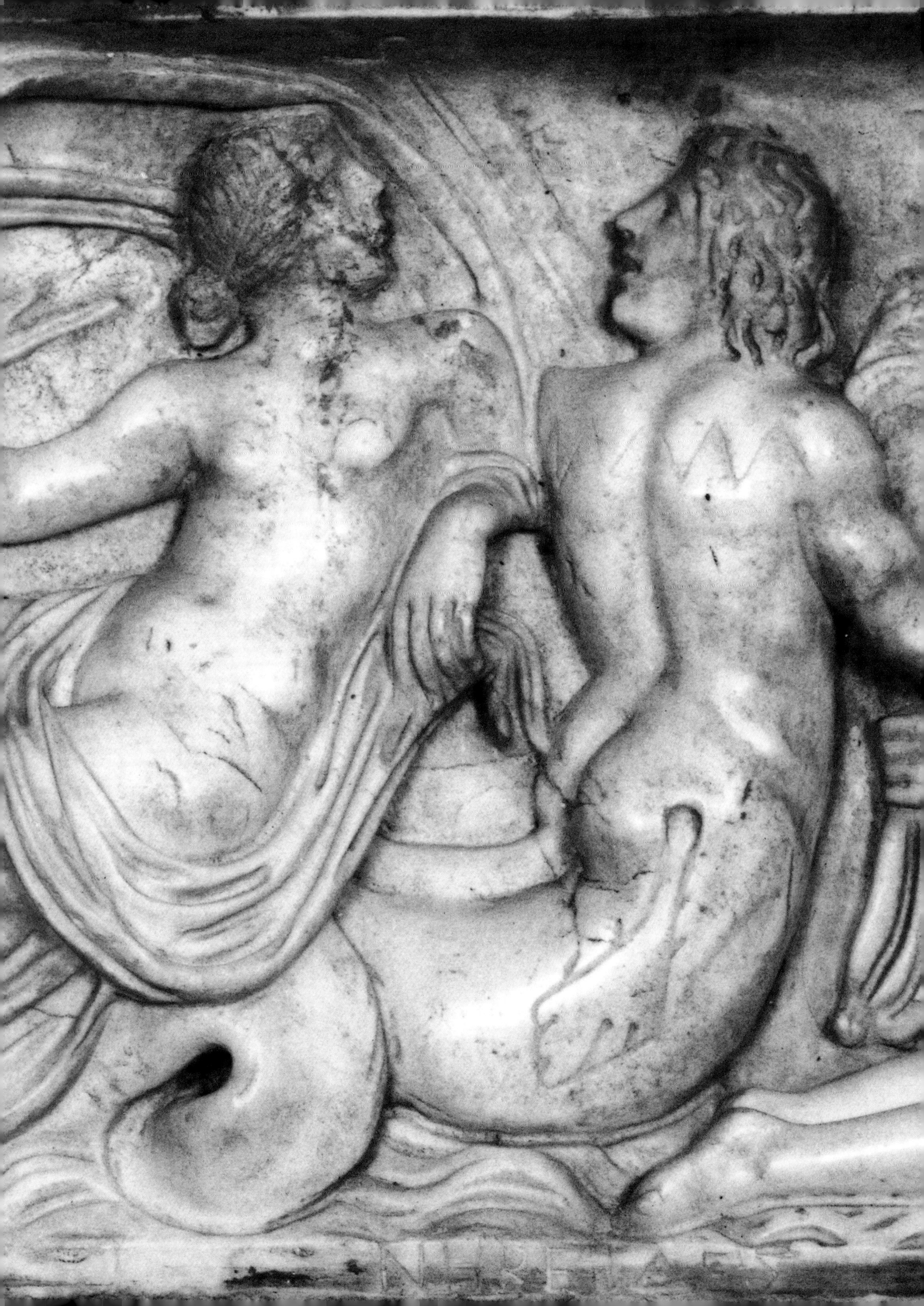

OPPOSITE:
Unknown, Roman, second century CE, *Sarcophagus Fragment: Eros with Nereids and Tritons* (detail), about 140–160 CE, marble, Acquisitions Fund, Hood Museum of Art; S.977.21